speakout 2ND EDITION

Advanced Plus
Workbook

without key

Richard Storton

CONTENTS

CONTENTS

GAME-CHANGERS

VOCABULARY

TRANSFORMATION

1 Add letters to complete the phrases in the sentences.

1 The results of the election s_ _ in m_ _ _ _ _ _ a chain of events which altered the nature of politics within most European democracies.

2 The university research team was pleased to announce a m_ _ _ _ b_ _ _ _ _ _ _ _ _ _ _ _ _ in their studies of the human genome.

3 She was considered a p_ _ _ _ _ _ within ecology studies – very few people initially shared her views on environmental protection.

4 C_ _ _ _ _ _ _ _ _ _ _ w_ _ _ _ _ in politics says that anyone younger than thirty is unlikely to be given a decisive role in government.

5 Their new design was potentially g_ _ _ -c_ _ _ _ _ _ _. Up to that point, few people had used grapene in building design.

6 Innovations in 3D printing had a p_ _ _ _ _ _ _ i_ _ _ _ _ on the way design companies could deliver prototypes to the market.

7 Researchers are conducting p_ _ _ _ _ s_ _ _ _ _ _ into ways of storing solar energy within wearable devices.

8 The publication of their results led to a p_ _ _ _ _ _ _ s_ _ _ _ in ways of assessing and calculating life expectancy.

LISTENING

2 A ▶ 1.1 Listen to an extract from a lecture on game-changing technologies. Complete the table as you listen.

Designer	What is it?	How does it work?
Talib Alhinai		
Solveiga Pakštaitė		
Sam Stranks		

B Listen again and complete the sentences with the exact words you hear. Use no more than three words.

1 Talib Alhinai's invention has the potential to quickly create _____ in areas hit by natural disasters.

2 Long-term, the innovation may also be utilised in the construction process when _____.

3 Mimica Touch was designed as a response to the creation of mass food waste and has a _____ on those who grow or sell foodstuffs.

4 Solveiga Pakštaitė's Mimica Touch product may signal significant changes in _____.

5 Sam Stranks' invention, perovskite, is produced by mixing man-made, low-cost and _____ materials.

6 As perovskite can be produced in different colours it has an _____ and _____.

C Match the underlined words from the recording with the definitions a)–f). Read the audio script on page 64 to help you.

1 Working in the field of aerial robotics, he has designed a <u>prototype</u> for a flying robot …

2 … another layer of plastic with <u>protuberances</u> and a final, smooth layer of plastic.

3 … reducing the <u>incidence</u> of workplace accidents.

4 He and a team based at MIT have been developing lightweight, efficient and <u>malleable</u> solar conductors …

5 … when bumps become <u>detectable</u> this indicates that the food product has gone bad.

6 … areas of the developing world which are currently energy <u>deficient</u>.

a) able to to be shaped without breaking

b) a rate of occurrence

c) able to be discovered or noticed

d) something from which copies are made

e) not having enough of something

f) something that sticks out from something else

GRAMMAR

VERB PATTERNS

3 Find and correct the mistakes in sentences 1–8. There are two mistakes in each sentence.

1 Have you ever considered to apply for a position in their research unit? If you're ready dedicate the time to it, it's a worthwhile role.

_____

2 Did you manage finding that article on renewable energy studies? I mean print it off for you last week.

_____

3 I regret telling you that unfortunately your application has failed this time. You could consider to reapply next year.

_____

4 Despite a setback he went on studying at the University of Gothenburg, where his research leading to a major breakthrough in geophysics.

_____

5 She's considered being one of the leading professionals in her field. I can't help to wonder just how she manages to do so much.

_____

6 After their first failure, they needed coming up with an alternative approach. Eventually, they decided launch a more compact drone.

_____

7 It's always been my goal doing something like this. You can't blame me for try something different at this point in life.

_____

8 Investors had committed spending several million on the pilot project. Sadly, it has a long way going before it's commercially viable.

_____

4 Complete the article with the correct form of the verbs in brackets.

VOCABULARY PLUS

PREPOSITIONAL PHRASES AFTER NOUNS

5 Complete the sentences with the nouns in the box and the correct preposition.

> aim   consequence   course   hesitation   hope
> implications   motivation   necessity   passion
> risk   success   talent

1 One _____ the government's recent policy change is that many academics can't continue funding their research.

2 She's always had a _____ cycling, so she jumped at the opportunity to do the Tour de France route.

3 He certainly shows a _____ fundraising – since we took him on, our donations have increased fourfold.

4 Alain lost weight and discovered a love of running in the _____ taking part in a six-week sports challenge at work.

5 I wonder what her _____ changing jobs was? I always thought she enjoyed her role.

6 There's no _____ getting me to do something like that! It's much too risky!

7 The _____ our campaign is to raise awareness about the issue of child poverty.

8 I would have absolutely no _____ recommending his book – it's unbelievably inspiring.

9 Despite knowing the _____ working in the area, a huge number of medical professionals volunteered to help out.

10 The _____ their report were wide-ranging. They signalled a paradigm shift in thinking.

11 We had considerable _____ encouraging young women to take up scientific subjects for study.

12 The majority of people recognise the _____ increased investment in health and education.

●●● ‹ ›   🔍 🏠

| HOME | STORIES | PHOTOS |

I'd like to think that my main motivation for doing this is
¹_____ (make) a difference to people's lives. But I suppose ²_____ (come) here was about ³_____ (try) something new that would really test me in terms of my ability. My role is ⁴_____ (identify) viable wild seed varieties. These are used ⁵_____ (create) genetically strengthened crop forms that will survive drought or flood conditions. Collectors go to great lengths ⁶_____ (gather) the seed.

One of our biggest challenges is securing financial support for projects. While many people want to donate to charities for life-threatening illnesses, they don't seem to think it's worth ⁷_____ (fund) the kind of things we do. Fortunately, there are a number of grants available which enable us ⁸_____ (continue) our research whilst

⁹_____ (teach) interns ¹⁰_____ (analyse) raw data from the experiments. This helps speed up the whole process.

Initially, I was a bit overawed by the level of ability here. Some of the graduates are capable of ¹¹_____ (do) things that many scientists will never achieve in a lifetime. It's game-changing stuff. Working with such an amazing team of committed professionals can't fail ¹²_____ (make) an impression. To be honest, it's hard to imagine myself ¹³_____ (do) anything other than this.

♡ 💬

VOCABULARY

ADJECTIVES: *NEEDING* AND *GIVING*

1 Complete the sentences with the adjectives in the box.

> altruistic   compassionate
> destitute   hard up   lavish
> on welfare   philanthropic
> unstinting   vulnerable

1 She was renowned as one of the most _____ individuals in the country – her annual donations surpassed those of many organisations.

2 After months of living on the streets, he was extremely _____ and in need of medical attention.

3 We were always taught to be _____ towards others, and to value what privileges we had.

4 After the family business failed, they were left completely _____.

5 I'm a bit _____ this month, but once my next payment comes through I'll be a bit more flush.

6 They are really _____ with their gifts – it's sometimes a bit embarrassing.

7 As we are all aware from previous charity campaigns, the people in this area are _____ in their generosity.

8 Don't think that they are doing that out of wholly _____ motives – they get tax relief on charitable donations.

9 Sadly, many of the children in the community are from broken homes and the family is living _____. We need to stop this cycle of poverty.

READING

2 A Read the article and choose the best title.

a) Social enterprise – what's in it for me?

b) Social enterprise – a worthwhile way to make money?

c) Social enterprise – who's really helping who?

Every so often, a new buzzword takes the business world by storm. A paradigm shift in how things are done, or a whole new lexicon of <u>abstruse</u> terms to tie the novice's head in knots. In recent years, one such concept that has gained considerable traction is social enterprise. Social enterprises are businesses which champion the honourable intention of changing the world for the better. By selling goods and services in the open market, social enterprises generate profits which are then reinvested in the local, or indeed global, community. The aim is to tackle social problems, improve opportunities and address inequality, among others. Evidently, the best way to secure the financial support and ongoing <u>allegiance</u> of millennial consumers is to care. Really care.

Putting this cynicism aside, is social enterprise actually something which makes a difference? High-profile social enterprises like Toms, which has grown in scope since its <u>inception</u>, have donated over 75 million pairs of new shoes to needy children around the globe, using a one-for-one business basis. For every pair of shoes sold, one is donated, enabling children to have improved health and safer access to education. With a decent pair of shoes, they can avoid any potential injuries on the walk to school – where possession of a pair can be an entry requirement. But there is also an array of other, smaller, initiatives which are doing their bit to build a better future.

Companies like Tarjimly run by Atif Javed, an MIT graduate, are making a difference too. Tarjimly instantly connects refugees, NGOs and immigrants in need of essential translation services – such as medical or legal aid – to translators around the world. While this service goes some way to addressing a real need in current climes, Javed explains their true aim is to be a 'world-class technology company for social good . . . pushing the boundaries of language and refugee research'. Leila Janah, founder of Samasource has <u>laudable goals</u>, too. Samasource helps to provide jobs to marginalised women and young people in impoverished areas, connecting low-income job seekers to dignified work in big name technology companies. The company has also branched out to create Samaschool, an organisation that provides low-income individuals with digital skills training.

While these examples are inspiring, and offer a vision of corporate caring that is hard not to warm to, it's perfectly reasonable to have reservations about the philosophy as a whole. There is certainly a growing trend for companies that have never really shown much compassion suddenly jumping on the impact investment bandwagon. If you have long been perceived as a <u>rapacious</u> multinational focused on profit above people, then one of the best ways to redress the balance is to show a big heart.

There are a number of high-profile companies who have partnered with NGOs and charitable organisations to ensure that their hard-earned dollars are invested into a whole <u>plethora</u> of needy causes. These tend to be extremely well-publicised initiatives, news of which often takes <u>precedence</u> over concerns about working conditions or corporate accountability. In fact, many business advisors highly recommend the social enterprise route to change negative public perceptions.

So, perhaps this is a clever idea that can shield large corporations from criticism by offering an air of <u>respectability</u>. But, if in the end it's people who benefit from this philanthropy, do such moral dilemmas matter?

B Read the article again. Choose the correct answer a), b), c) or d) according to the text.

1 What view of big business does the writer express in the first paragraph?
  a) It frequently reinvents itself in order to remain important.
  b) It firmly positions itself as being vital to community development.
  c) It has a tendency to latch on to concepts for its own benefit.
  d) It has a forward-thinking approach to sustainable causes.

2 In the second paragraph, what point does the writer make?
  a) Only large-scale enterprises have the ability to make an impact on social issues.
  b) Lower profile social enterprises can also make a difference.
  c) Only well-publicised enterprises have the ability to effect social change.
  d) Social enterprises need to have a broad vision to be successful.

3 The writer highlights examples of social enterprises which
  a) focus specifically on access to employment.
  b) have a purely charitable agenda.
  c) focus on addressing issues of social integration.
  d) have a purely profit-driven agenda.

4 In the fouth paragraph, the writer points out that
  a) interest in social enterprise is a niche market.
  b) interest in social enterprises has become more mainstream.
  c) social enterprise is always of interest to the public.
  d) social enterprise is a philosophical approach to business.

5 In the fifth paragraph, the writer says that large corporations
  a) assume the role of social enterprise to avoid closer scrutiny.
  b) assume the role of social enterprise to increase profits.
  c) assume the role of social enterprise for tax purposes.
  d) assume the role of social enterprise to do good.

6 A recurring idea in the whole article is that social enterprise
  a) is a positive force when truly practised with good intentions.
  b) is a temporary solution to highly complex, bigger issues.
  c) is sometimes initiated for questionable reasons.
  d) has provided a viable alternative to conventional wisdom.

C Match the underlined words from the article with the definitions.

1 loyalty or commitment to a group or cause
2 ideas which are obscure or difficult to understand
3 aggressively greedy or grasping
4 a quality of being socially acceptable
5 being considered more important than something else
6 aims which are deserving of praise
7 the establishment or starting point of something
8 a large or excessive amount

D Write your own ideas on the question raised at the end of the article.

GRAMMAR
CONTINUOUS AND PERFECT ASPECT

3 Underline the correct alternative to complete the sentences.

1 So, how long *are you having / have you had / have you been having* fundraising events like this? *Are you raising / Have you raised / Have you been raising* as much as you had hoped?

2 On their arrival in Europe, the migrants *had travelled / have travelled / had been travelling* for up to three months. They *are hoping / have hoped / have been hoping* that their ordeal is now over.

3 I'm so bored, I *was standing / am standing / have been standing* on this street corner collecting money since 8a.m. I'll *be doing / 'll have been doing / 'll have done* door-to-door collections tomorrow night, too.

4 We were totally amazed by what people *have been donating / had donated* to the auction. We *are thinking / have thought / had thought* we would only raise a few hundred pounds, but I think it'll be much more.

5 By next week, our funding *will be increasing / will have increased / is increasing* to more than €10,000. We *have planned / are planning / have been planning* to spend the bulk of it on equipment for the park.

6 It's fantastic that she *is raising / has raised / has been raising* so much support for her campaign. It seems only a few days ago since we *were designing / have designed / have been designing* her web page.

4 For 1–6, complete the second sentence so it has a similar meaning to the first. Use no more than five words and the word given.

1 Donating online is new to me. NEVER
I _____ before.

2 Anna hasn't been to Japan before. FIRST
This is the _____ Japan.

3 The apartment will take us three weeks to renovate. RENOVATED
In three weeks' time _____ the apartment.

4 They rely on you too much. They have since their baby was born. BEEN
They _____ too much since the birth of their baby.

5 He meets charity commission officials on 17th June. WILL
He _____ officials from the charity commission on 17th June.

6 We spoke to every donor today. HAD
We _____ the end of the day.

Extending a hand of hope

Have you ever been in a situation when everything seemed ¹_____? Well, in times of need, it's worthwhile remembering that help could be close at hand. Help@Hand is a website which connects individuals in need with charitable organisations and provides them with opportunities to turn their lives around.

As website founder Andy Steele explains, 'Sometimes people come to us who have just ²_____. They can't see a way out from their current difficulties. We address that by actively seeking solutions.' His website can offer a ³_____ in these troubled times by matching people's needs with services that can readily assist them. One recipient of this help was medical student Orhan Demir. After completing his studies, he wanted to set up a small clinic. His ⁴_____ when he realised that his visa had expired, and that without a job offer he would ⁵_____ of staying in the country. His ⁶_____ was to try and find an employer fast. Help@Hand matched him with a charity that offered check-ups to the homeless and vulnerable. For Orhan, there is ⁷_____ that he'll one day be able to fulfil his ambition. For the charity, there is a skilled practitioner.

What makes Help@Hand an interesting proposition is that it isn't a charity solely focused on raising donations. The main approach is to ensure that those in need can work within part of a wider community to improve their lot. Charity groups have ⁸_____ that benefactors will continue to support this ground-breaking initiative, and Steele certainly has ⁹_____ that it will grow in scope.

WRITING

AN ARTICLE

5 A Complete the article above with collocations a)–i). Use a collocation dictionary if necessary.

a) hopes were dashed
b) given up hope
c) best hope
d) expressed hope
e) high hopes
f) glimmer of hope
g) have no hope
h) renewed hope
i) completely hopeless

B Read the features of informal articles. Which features has the writer used?

1 A catchy title
2 Informal rhetorical questions
3 A question-answer sequence
4 Addressing the reader directly
5 Quotations
6 Examples
7 Informal sentence starters
8 Contractions
9 Informal lexis and lexical phrases

C Underline the correct alternative to complete the collocations.

1 It's incredibly important that we *respect/reflect* the wishes of our patrons for privacy and keep their names anonymous.

2 She'd hoped that they would secure long-term funding for the project and finally *got/granted* her wish last week with the news of interested investors.

3 We can't afford to *ignore/express* the wishes of the general public at this critical stage in negotiations. They are vital to our success.

4 If I could *grant/get* one wish, it would be to make the world a safer place.

5 On the whole, I was pleased with the local council decision. It broadly *fulfilled/reflected* the wishes of local residents.

6 Joanna has *expressed/made* a wish to study in the United States. We're doing all we can to make that happen.

D Write an article of your own (250 words). Focus on a project you know about that is concerned with wishes or hopes. Use the article in Exercise 5A as a model.

E Read your first draft and then find the nouns (including synonyms) that appear frequently. Use a collocation dictionary to vary the verbs and adjectives that collocate with those nouns.

VOCABULARY

COLLOCATIONS

1 Match words from boxes A and B to make collocations to complete the sentences.

A

access business collaborative on-demand online outer profit sharing umbrella

B

access consumption driven economy (x2) fringes model terms transactions

1 Their business model is completely _____. Their only desire is to increase their annual turnover.

2 While companies like Uber could be regarded as pioneers in the _____, some of their business practices may be questionable.

3 As they have little to do with sharing of any resources, it would be better to refer to them as proponents of the _____.

4 Over the last few years, there has been a sharp increase in the number of _____ being made. It may be due to consumer confidence in cyber-security.

5 When Airbnb launched the idea of _____, where both organisations and individuals could benefit from business transactions, this appealed to many apartment owners.

6 They have an incredibly successful _____. The value of their company has more than trebled in recent years.

7 While a number of businesses will accept Bitcoins for services, it still remains a currency on the _____ of the economy.

8 The entertainment industry has been revolutionised by the concept of _____. Overheads can be reduced, while the range of products available to consumers grows.

9 'Intellectual property' is one of those _____ which is often mentioned in contracts. It simply refers to certain exclusive rights in intangible things.

FUNCTION

PRESENTING SURVEY RESULTS

2 Put the words in the correct order to complete the conversations.

1 A: What was your view on why the companies were so successful?
B: impression / that / simply / was /my
Well, _____
they offer great customer service.

2 A: Do most people agree the sharing economy is a good thing?
B: that / the / seems / be / to / consensus.
Well, _____. It's here to stay, if nothing else.

3 A: Can you explain why there are fewer subscribers now?
B: speculate / might / one / that
Well, _____ it's due to growing competition within the industry.

4 A: Did you find that most people enjoyed their experience of using the service?
B: whole / the / on
Yes, _____ they were very positive indeed.

5 A: Did you say that demographics plays a big part in their business profile?
B: this / illustration / of / another
Yes, _____ is that the online interface is more youth-oriented.

6 A: Don't people buy films from their database, too?
B: speaking / though / generally
Yes, but _____
its commercial focus is on streaming content.

7 A: Can you tell us a bit more about customer complaints?
B: example / one / cite / to
Well, _____, a user complained that choice could be limited.

LEARN TO

CHUNK LANGUAGE

3 A Mark with / where you would pause in the following sentence if you read it aloud.

Another illustration of this is the number of people between the ages of eighteen and twenty-five who applied for tax relief but who as it happened hadn't paid any tax.

B ▶ 1.2 Listen and check.

C Read the extract and mark with / for a short pause, and // for a longer pause.

Does it really matter whether businesses have a social agenda as long as they are benefiting the economy? Many people may believe that in an increasingly globalised world we should be more philanthropic that is caring. However there's no point in speaking of doing this if nobody's quality of life improves is there?

D ▶ 1.3 Listen and check.

2 LEARNING

VOCABULARY

LEARNING

1 Complete the sentences with the words and phrases in the box.

> crucial element   derided
> engaged   highly beneficial
> make an educated guess
> praised   steer clear of
> something of a perfectionist

1 Their method of teaching, once _____ by critics, has now become part of the mainstream education experience in many countries.

2 You may not know the answer, but if you _____, there's always the chance you'll get it right.

3 She's a very competent speaker, but there are some topics she tends to _____. Perhaps she feels uncomfortable with them.

4 There's a lot of evidence pointing towards learner independence being the _____ in successful language study.

5 It's so important that students remain as _____ as possible. They'll be more motivated that way.

6 Reading to a child from an early age is _____ to their educational development.

7 I was always _____ by my parents when I did well at school, but they supported me when I found things tough, too.

8 He's _____ – it takes him forever to finish redrafting essays.

LISTENING

2 A Look at the photos. What might people enjoy about learning to do these things?

B ▶ 2.1 Listen and check.

C Listen to the two extracts again. For questions 1–4, choose the answer a), b) or c) which fits best according to what you hear.

Extract 1

You hear a woman talking about a course that she attends.

1 What is the woman doing when she mentions the cost of classes?
   a) highlighting their accessibility
   b) criticising their exclusivity
   c) justifying the expense

2 What advice does she give for prospective participants?
   a) Don't expect instant results.
   b) Avoid making mistakes.
   c) Accept assistance wherever possible.

Extract 2

You hear a tutor talking about the value of learning to play an instrument.

3 He believes that people's opinion about arts subjects
   a) is overly critical.
   b) is too simplistic.
   c) is informed by long-standing attitudes.

4 When talking about introducing the guitar to schoolchildren he reveals
   a) his concern about their lack of enthusiasm.
   b) his delight at their reactions.
   c) his dismay that they have few opportunities to be creative.

D Match the underlined words and phrases from the recording with definitions a)–f). Read the audio script on page 64 to help you.

1 ... over time numbers have <u>dwindled</u>.
2 I've had more opportunity to <u>grill</u> the instructor ...
3 Having said that, seniors and the unemployed are <u>subsidised</u>.
4 I wouldn't want to <u>cast aspersions</u> on head teachers ...
5 ... cutting back on <u>itinerant</u> teachers who offer art or music lessons.
6 All the attitude <u>drops away</u>, and they just start having fun.

a) disappears
b) have costs reduced by helping pay for a service
c) ask lots of detailed questions
d) to make critical or unpleasant remarks
e) moving from place to place
f) become gradually less or smaller

GRAMMAR
IF AND RELATED EXPRESSIONS

3 Complete the article with the words in the box.

as long as   but for   if any   if in doubt

as long as   but for   if any   if in doubt
if so   it seems as if   otherwise
provided that   rarely, if ever   unless
whether or not   without

Home   **News**   **Articles**   **Listings**

A quick glance through any number of online forums will reveal that for the pedagogical community, learning styles are a fairly ubiquitous concept. While there's an abundance of research into the field, 1 _____ there is little consensus on what learning styles are. 2 _____ do two commentators seem to agree. In fact, some educational experts actually argue they don't exist. 3 _____, that would certainly contradict a good deal of official policy.

The traditional view is that each learner has a particular favoured style which enables them to pick up information more effectively than other forms of teaching and learning. Conventional wisdom would have it that 4 _____ children learn regularly in their chosen style, they will have a better chance of success. 5 _____, they may not fulfil their potential.

6 _____ recent studies by cognitive psychologists, this might be viewed as a given. However, they have shown that students don't perform any differently 7 _____ they are given tests in one learning style or another. What they may have, rather than a particular style, is a preference. So, what issues, 8 _____, does this raise? Well, the problem has been that over time, what began as a notion has become a theory of the mind which has been used to justify curricula. 9 _____, take a look at some of the materials rigorously imposed upon teachers and students.

Critics of more entrenched approaches to learning styles would argue that while people do learn differently, it's important to say how they learn differently and to focus on meaningful difference which can be observed. They would posit that 10 _____ learning contexts are addressed, styles are fairly meaningless. 11 _____ we think about a bigger picture, we can better address needs. 12 _____ looking at the learning environment, and factors which impact on it, we can't start to make real, measurable differences.

4 For 1–8, complete the second sentence so it has a similar meaning to the first. Use no more than five words and the word given.

1 She'll be accepted at her first choice of university, but only if she passes the exams. PROVIDED
Her first-choice university _____ she passes the exams.

2 Apparently, there are a few questions about the accuracy of last year's tests. SEEMS
It _____ some inaccuracies in last year's tests.

3 It's not that clear if he learnt much during his degree. WHETHER
I don't _____ he learnt anything during his degree.

4 If you're not sure what to do, send an email to your tutor. DOUBT
I'd contact _____.

5 There's very little difference in the colleges, really. ANY
There is little _____ the two colleges.

6 If you put in a bit more effort, I can't see you failing. AS
You'll _____ you put in a bit more effort.

7 If it's true, we should tell somebody. SO
_____ be told.

8 They almost never attended the lectures I was at. IF
They _____ to the same lectures as me.

VOCABULARY *PLUS*
IDIOMS: FEELINGS

5 Match the sentence halves.

1 As soon as I walked into class, I got that sinking feeling;
2 I'm sorry, I don't think I'll make it to today's lesson;
3 If you ask me, he's got a bit of a chip on his shoulder;
4 If you applied to study there, they'd welcome you with open arms;
5 The teaching union has its back to the wall;
6 When I got to university, I felt like a fish out of water;
7 I've been on cloud nine since I received the news;
8 The education policy looks to be coming apart at the seams;

a) I really can't believe that they've accepted my application.
b) I think he feels inferior because of where he studied.
c) they are under pressure to negotiate with the government.
d) I'm feeling a bit under the weather.
e) everyone seemed so much more confident than me.
f) everyone's asking how the government intends to provide funding.
g) the desks were laid out for a test and I hadn't done any revision.
h) you're just the kind of student they want to enrol.

VOCABULARY

COLLOCATIONS: EDUCATION

1 Adjust the underlined words to make the correct collocations.

1 The emphasis at our college is on <u>finding</u> _____ your potential.

2 There is a new interactive space for learning, and many students are <u>fulfilling</u> _____ the initiative by recording their presentations.

3 We have always had <u>striving</u> _____ standards, but that doesn't mean that in <u>focus</u> _____ for excellence we ignore what makes learners unique.

4 While we encourage everyone to work as hard as possible, there is a <u>nurturing</u> _____ on individuality: students can set their own long-term goals and learning pathway.

5 We're quite flexible as a school. Although we do offer a <u>mutual</u> _____ curriculum, we're not all that results-driven.

6 We're interested in our students fostering <u>quality</u> _____ relationships. Once they have <u>good</u> _____ respect for one another, you're on your way to helping them attain what they need in life.

READING

2 Read the article. For questions 1–10, choose from the sections (A–D). The sections may be chosen more than once.

Which section ...

1 gives reasons why forest schools help child development?

2 cites a psychological term for a condition affecting some young people?

3 warns of pursuing an education system without a focus on working together?

4 mentions forest schools being used for children who may have behavioural issues?

5 expresses concerns that some people have about the forest school system?

6 highlights the dangers of limiting childrens' natural instincts?

7 describes some beneficial life skills?

8 criticises a view which it considers to be outmoded?

9 mentions the potential for using forest schools more broadly?

10 draws attention to a disadvantage of more traditional teaching environments?

●●● ◁ ▷

A

There is a growing amount of concern from many academics in the study of education that children are suffering from a lack of engagement with nature and the outdoor environment. What has been dubbed 'nature deficit disorder' can be characterised by a sense of alienation from surroundings that results in a diminished use of the senses, attention difficulties and higher rates of physical or emotional illness. Furthermore, children who fail to engage with the natural world through play or outdoor learning are often seen to have an inability to assess risk. To address such concerns, forest schools have often been promoted as an educational alternative to more traditional classroom-based learning models. Currently, many forest school programmes tend to focus on early years, or disaffected pupils; however, there is evidence that such projects have noticeable benefits for children across the learning spectrum.

B

So, why does a forest school ethos make a difference? Well, for one, there's that exploration of risk, which many development psychologists highlight as an essential stage in learning. Children have a natural need for risk-taking, and exposure to reasonable uncertainty in a controlled environment provides the opportunity to feed this. Without such opportunities, as can be offered in an outdoor learning space, a child may well pursue unmanaged risk in a non-educational environment. Dealing with hazardous situations helps to develop personality traits such as resilience and self-reliance. More conventional classroom spaces tend to limit the opportunity for risk-taking, thereby stifling a sense of learner independence.

C

As important as independence is, success in adulthood is most often aligned with collaboration and critical thinking. For forest schools to work, they also rely upon the communal approach. Individuals may interact with the natural world to engage interests and develop mental and physical well-being, but they do this as part of a broader team. It's not enough just to have pupils doing traditional lessons in a non-traditional environment. Or to only foster a sense of connection with nature. They also need to embrace the outdoor learning space as a locus of social interaction, too.

D

There are, of course, critics of any approach which goes against the norms. Having said that, these tend to either focus on the pro-environmental stance of forest schooling, or raise concerns regarding the prospective hygiene of outdoor learning. While the latter may be a valid point, it has been noted that childen participating in forest schools tend to have better attendance records when illness is taken into account. It may be that pupils tend not to be in extremely close proximity, and so illness doesn't spread. General cleanliness may be an issue, depending on the location of the outdoor learning space, but on the whole this can be monitored as well as in a conventional school. The notion that a pro-environmental perspective is somehow a drawback is much more contentious. Given that young people will become the stewards of our environment, and involved in making the policy that shapes it, it seems remiss not to encourage any interest they may harbour.

GRAMMAR
NOMINAL RELATIVE CLAUSES

3 Complete the texts with the words in the box.

> how   what   whatever   whichever
> whoever   why

The secret to good learning?

A Learning is all about collaboration.
[1]_____ you work with, you can always glean some extra piece of knowledge. It might be technical know-how, or just a more streamlined approach to completing a more mundane task, but anything that you learn from colleagues is worthwhile. I also think it's essential to be open about any difficulties you're facing. If I'm not sure [2]_____ to do, I'll ask – there's little point trying to conceal inadequacies, because they'll always come out in the end. [3]_____ mistakes you make, can always be turned into learning opportunities.

B The best ways to learn? I suppose a lot depends on [4]_____ learning style you prefer. Although I think you need to consider [5]_____ you are learning, too. So often we make educational demands where the outcomes are unclear. I think that lack of clarity obscures things. If teachers took more time to weigh up [6]_____ the knowledge that they were imparting would be of use to their pupils, it would be a good start.

4 For 1–6, write the second sentence so it has a similar meaning to the first. Use the words given.

1 Can you remember the subject of our discussion last week?
recall / what / was / talk
_____

2 I always thought that life at university would be like this.
how / imagined / be
_____

3 She thinks I'm always making mistakes.
According / whatever / do / wrong
_____

4 If something happens, you'll be to blame.
Anything / that / wrong
_____

5 He only gave me a very small amount of information.
told / what / little
_____

6 There are so many good classes, choosing one is hard.
know / which / choose
_____

WRITING
TAKING NOTES; WRITING A SUMMARY

5 A ▶ 2.2 Listen to an interview about the nature of teaching. Complete the notes.

> **Issues within teaching**
>
> Workload = problematic
> Classroom focus vs ongoing intellectual development
> Classroom teaching hours:
> England – [1]_____   OECD average [2]_____
> Japan – 2ndry school Ts = 32 percent class time. But standards v. high.
> No time for [3]_____
> ∴ less [4]_____
> Need – role to develop, opp to explore field, etc.
> **Out-of-class time**
> Currently – [5]_____ focused
> Ideal – more opps for collaboration with
> [6]_____
> **Other concerns**
> Pay [7]_____

B Read the summary. Has the writer
- used paragraphs for each topic?
- included the relevant information based on the notes?
- used discourse markers or cohesive devices to link ideas?
- used their own words in a concise way?
- used any statistics to support information?
- a) summarised in an objective way or b) given an opinion?

In my opinion, one of the current problems facing the teaching profession in the UK is that in recent years there has been a considerable increase in the workload. With newly-qualified teachers being asked to spend more time in the classroom teaching, there is less opportunity for them to develop the skills they need to become better teachers. In the UK, teachers can spend much longer than the OECD average in class. Contrastively, Japanese secondary school teachers spend a lot less time in class. Meanwhile, this hasn't affected standards, which remain very high.

However, the situation is very different in the UK, the profession is certainly less intellectually attractive to graduates. Where there is currently provision of out-of-class time, this tends to be allocated to administrative tasks. If teachers could spend more time working with colleagues and observing other teachers' classrooms while also preparing materials collectively, or even working with parents, then I believe that would make a tremendous difference to the role. This model is considered best practice in the highest performing education systems – Japan, South Korea, Finland.

C Write your own summary of the interview in Exercise 5A (200 words). Use the checklist in Exercise 5B to help you.

VOCABULARY

CREATIVITY

1 Complete the pairs of sentences with the correct word or phrase.

1 fertile / vivid
  a) She has such a _____ imagination – so far, she's written more than ten novels.
  b) He's always had a _____ imagination – he's forever making up stories about things.

2 heart / rote
  a) Many students rely on _____ learning to pass their exams.
  b) I remember spending hours at school having to learn poems by _____.

3 intuition / intellect
  a) As the study was inconclusive we had to rely on _____ rather then detailed analysis.
  b) He's fairly lazy, and often relies on _____ rather than hard work to achieve good grades.

4 tried and tested / think outside the box
  a) I'd prefer to go with a _____ method. It's safer that way.
  b) Sometimes you need to _____ – there might be an alternative approach.

5 rigid / versatile
  a) They seem to have a particularly _____ mindset – they don't like to do anything out of the ordinary.
  b) The course offers a _____ approach to learning, combining conversation, video lessons and exchange programmes.

FUNCTION

LEADING A DISCUSSION

2 A Read the extracts from discussions about education and creativity. Find and correct two mistakes in each extract.

1 A: So, our task today is to discuss creative approaches to educational improvement. Who'd like to kick this one out? Sally?
  B: Yeah, sure. Well, I've been looking at some of the ways attainment is being addressed at primary levels. Rather than traditional testing forms, students are being offered the opportunity to prepare task-focused work which highlights their learning.
  A: Could you illustrate on that?
  B: Well, the idea is that they work together to make or develop something which can show teachers what they've picked up during the academic year.

2 A: Tony, you mentioned schools specialising in one particular medium. Could you implore that further?
  B: Sure, there are situations where schools have developed partnerships with professionals in the creative industries to push a broader skills base. For instance, collaborating with a local radio station or gallery.
  A: I can't imagine that works. Students could get a lot out of that.
  B: Yeah, and it ties into a lot of subject areas – the arts, communication, ITC …

B ▶ 2.3 Listen and check.

LEARN TO

MANAGE INTERACTION

3 A Put the words in the correct order to complete the conversations.

1 A: Kate / anything / to / want / add / you / did?

  _____
  B: Yes, actually, I was wondering if you'd read the report on forest schools.

2 A: The main reason that the attainment gap is growing is lack of training.
  B: make / that / about / comment / a / can / I?

  _____

3 A: Substantially less is spent on teacher training than in the past.
  B: digressing / we / think / might / I / be …

  _____

4 A: up / I / wrap / just / what / was / I / can / saying?

  _____
  B: OK, but can you make it a quick point?

5 A: Well, I'm not convinced myself, I think …
  B: Paul / to / say / can / just / we / what / hear / wanted?

  _____

6 A: Look, there's a video about it online. I'll show you …
  B: move / on / we're / time / so / pressed / let's / for.

  _____

B ▶ 2.4 Listen and check.

C Listen again and repeat sentences 1–6 from Exercise 3A. Concentrate on the intonation to sound impatient, tentative or firm and polite.

GRAMMAR   VERB PATTERNS

1 For 1–10, complete the second sentence so it has a similar meaning to the first. Use no more than five words and the word given.

1 Ella succeeded in completing her application on time.
MANAGED
Ella _____ her application on time.

2 I think that this is the right place, here.
APPEARS
This _____ the right place.

3 It's really kind of you to help me with my essay.
APPRECIATE
I _____ me with the essay.

4 'Shall I get you a coffee, Kate?' said Tom.
OFFERED
Tom _____ Kate a coffee.

5 Getting the money meant we could continue our research.
ENABLED
Getting the money _____ with our research.

6 Parking is not permitted here.
ALLOWED
You are _____ here.

7 She might miss the plane if she waits.
RISKS
She _____ if she waits.

8 It's compulsory for all college employees to carry ID.
REQUIRED
All college employees _____ carry ID.

9 We can't be angry with him – he wants to try a new job.
BLAMED
He shouldn't _____ to try a new job.

10 It was agreed that the issue would be brought up at the next meeting.
BRING
They resolved _____ up at the following meeting.

VOCABULARY   REVIEW 1

2 Complete the pairs of sentences with the correct word or phrase.

1 had a profound impact on / set in motion
a) His discovery _____ changes in the way that people conducted research.
b) Her approach to playing _____ many younger composers, who were inspired by her.

2 altruistic / compassionate
a) He might seem generous, but it's not for _____ reasons; he gets course credits for voluntary work.
b) She's an incredibly _____ individual. She cared for her parents for years.

3 outer fringe / umbrella term
a) I'd consider digital marketing an _____ as there are so many varieties labouring under that description.
b) They've been operating on the _____ of business for years. Who knows if what they do is actually legal.

4 game-changer / pioneer
a) In terms of promoting renewables, the new lithium ion battery was a _____.
b) With her unconventional style, she's widely regarded as a _____ in the fashion industry.

5 business model / online transaction
a) I'm afraid I don't have much confidence in their _____. It seems very vague.
b) I understand that our _____ to cover the bill didn't go through.

6 destitute / hard up
a) I can't wait for pay day to arrive. I'm a bit _____ at the moment.
b) Following the banking crisis, millions of people were left _____.

7 access economy / on-demand access
a) The _____ has opened up a world of possibilities for people who want to make a little bit more money.
b) The film was only available via _____, and we don't have a subscription.

8 unstinting / vulnerable
a) With tax increases hitting hard, many people are becoming _____ to poverty.
b) She showed _____ energy and enthusiasm throughout the charity campaign.

9 pilot studies / paradigm shift
a) They conducted several _____ to determine how efficient the system was.
b) The advent of motion capture technology was a _____ for film-making.

10 lavish / philanthropic
a) I really wish they wouldn't be so _____ with presents. It must cost a fortune.
b) She's renowned for her _____ works. She donates a great deal to charity.

GRAMMAR CONTINUOUS AND PERFECT ASPECT

3 Complete the text with the correct form of the verbs in brackets.

Since we arrived here in the summer we
¹_____ (wonder) how best to help
the community. The locals ²_____
(be) so welcoming, and we just want to give something
back, you know? A couple of weeks ago, we started
an online campaign for the local school. We
³_____ (set up) a website
where people can make donations. But unlike most
fundraising drives, they'll be donating time, rather
then money. So far, we ⁴_____
(have) a lot of interest from different tradespeople,
and even the media. On Friday morning I
⁵_____ (speak) to local radio
about the project. A bit nerve-wracking, but hopefully
it'll go well. Kate ⁶_____ (arrange)
things with all the different businesses who want to
get involved – it ⁷_____ (take) up
most of her time at the moment. To be
honest, we ⁸_____ (amaze) by
everyone's unstinting generosity. At the beginning,
we ⁹_____ (think) perhaps
fifty or so hours would be donated, but it
¹⁰_____ (look) more like three
hundred at this point. It just feels like a short time
since we ¹¹_____ (discuss) the
idea, and now it really ¹²_____
(take) off.

VOCABULARY *PLUS*
PREPOSITIONAL PHRASES AFTER NOUNS

4 Underline the correct alternatives.

1 He was only young when we discovered he had an incredible talent *for/of* mathematics.
2 One key consequence *on/of* their policy has been a growth in class sizes.
3 It's worth remembering that the implications *of/in* this plan failing are massive.
4 If you ask me, he lacks the motivation *for/of* such an important role.
5 We had no hesitation *in/on* accepting their generous offer.
6 They started their business with the aim *for/of* providing a bespoke service to clients.
7 Since last year, we've had considerable success *for/in* extending our sales reach.
8 You shouldn't ignore the necessity *in/of* a reliable mountain guide.
9 It was during a trip to Australia that I developed a passion *for/in* surfing.
10 The rescue team have been searching for days. There's no hope *of/in* them finding anyone.

FUNCTION PRESENTING SURVEY RESULTS

5 Complete the conversations with the phrases in the box.

> another illustration of this   might speculate that
> my impression was   on the whole
> that seems to be the consensus   to cite one example

1 **A:** Have you found that most customers are happy with the service?
   B: Yes, _____ – although there are always going to be a few issues.
2 **A:** Do they offer any advantage in terms of service?
   B: Well, _____ they will deliver anywhere seven days a week.
3 **A:** That's pretty useful. I guess it helps more flexible small businesses.
   B: Yes, _____ is that they offer a packaging service, too.
4 **A:** Why did people use that company over others?
   B: Well, _____ they offered more competive prices than anyone else.
5 **A:** Are people concerned about the lengths of contracts they have to sign up to?
   B: I think _____ customers I spoke to were happy with six-month contracts.
6 **A:** Can you give us a reason why there are so many businesses like this starting up?
   B: Well, you _____ it's because there's less regulation in the market these days.

VOCABULARY REVIEW 2

6 Complete the text with the words and phrases in the box.

> derided   engaged   fire imagination
> fufill potential   mutual respect   quality curriculum
> rigorous standards   steer clear of
> think outside the box

I think that the reason so many educational
policies are ¹_____ is that
they tend to be quick-fix political decisions,
rather than looking at what is needed to keep
young people ²_____
in learning. All that most people want is that
their kids get the opportunity to ³_____
their _____ – they aren't all particularly
concerned about attainment and assessment. Yes,
there need to be ⁴_____ to
ensure that teaching is of the highest level, but
we ought to ⁵_____ telling
teachers what to do all the time. Anyone who can
⁶_____ should be encouraged
to explore this creative facet. As long as there's a
⁷_____, there should be some
flexibility on how it's delivered. A good teacher will
be able to ⁸_____ and foster a
sense of ⁹_____ among pupils.

GRAMMAR   *IF* AND RELATED EXPRESSIONS

7 Complete the conversations with the phrases in the box. You do not need all the phrases and sometimes more than one answer is possible.

> as long as   but for   if any   if in doubt   if so
> it seemed as if   otherwise   provided that
> unless   without

1 **A:** You and your friends have just ordered a takeaway delivery. When it comes, no one has money on them. Do you pay?
  B: Not _____ they intend to contribute later on.

2 **A:** You're in a meeting, and your colleague, a friend, is making no sense. Everyone is getting frustrated. What would you do?
  B: I'd try to help him/her out, _____ I'm not acting like a friend, am I?

3 **A:** Would you ever consider studying abroad?
  B: Yes, _____ I had a place at a good university and enough money.

4 **A:** Would you ever walk out on someone during a date?
  B: Maybe. If _____ we just weren't going to click.

5 **A:** What would you do if you found a suitcase full of cash on a train?
  B: _____ I'd leave it where it was. And maybe tell someone at the next station.

6 **A:** Do you think he made much difference to the team?
  B: _____ his goals, we'd have been relegated this season.

VOCABULARY *PLUS*   FEELINGS

8 Add letters to complete the phrases in the sentences.

1 I wouldn't bother getting into a argument with him, he's got a c_ _ _ _ on his s_ _ _ _ _ _ _ about the fact that he didn't get the job.

2 He m_ _ _ _ my f_ _ _ _ c_ _ _ _ _ – I can't stand being in the same room as him.

3 If you ever change your mind about studying here, we'd w_ _ _ _ _ _ _ you with o_ _ _ a_ _ _.

4 I'm not sure that team sports are his thing; he looked like a f_ _ _ out of w_ _ _ _.

5 That's it, I'm heading home. I've felt u_ _ _ _ the w_ _ _ _ _ _ since last night.

6 Despite their good intentions, their plans began to come a_ _ _ _ at the s_ _ _ _.

7 You know that s_ _ _ _ _ _ _ f_ _ _ _ _ _ you get when you realise you've pressed send by mistake?

8 When I realised how close we'd come to danger, it made my b_ _ _ _ r_ _ c_ _ _.

GRAMMAR   NOMINAL RELATIVE CLAUSES

9 Underline the correct alternative in the sentences.

1 I think it's really important to discuss *whatever/ whichever* problems you've been having with your studies. That way you can make improvements.

2 I'll work with *whoever/however* I want to at the time. Learning is about collaborating with a range of different people.

3 I tend to read as much as possible; *whichever/ whenever* I find a good book, I can hardly put it down.

4 Learning a new language is always fun *however/ whatever* it happens. It can be a new phrase from a taxi driver, or something you pick up in a class.

5 When I find a synonym for a new word, I tend to use *whichever/whatever* is the easiest for me to pronounce, even though it might not work in the context.

6 There comes a certain point *where/when* you just need to take responsibility for your actions.

7 I feel that it's important to know *why/how* you intend to resolve the matter.

8 I'm sorry, I just don't know *how/what* to say about that.

FUNCTION   LEADING A DISCUSSION

10A Put the underlined words in the correct order to complete the sentences.

a) can / just / come / in / if / I / here, I've got a few ideas.

b) want / anything / add / to / you / did, Pete?

c) might / we / be / digressing / I / think a bit.

d) make / comment / about / a / that / can / I, please?

e) focused / stay / let's; there's a lot to cover.

f) we're / on / for / move / so / pressed / let's / time, shall we?

B Complete the conversations with the sentences from Exercise 10A.

1 **A:** _____
  B: Good point, we've only got a few minutes before we report back to class.

2 **A:** Did anyone see that documentary about this issue on TV?
  B: _____; can we just answer the questions?

3 **A:** _____
  B: Yeah, I did actually. I think we need to look at other options, too.

4 **A:** _____
  B: Sure, what was it you wanted to say, Ella?

5 **A:** _____
  B: OK, we should try and stick to the main topic.

6 **A:** _____
  B: OK, but can you keep it brief, Anna?

CHECK

Circle the correct option to complete the sentences.

1 As far as I'm concerned, this idea is a _____.
  a) profound impact   **b)** game-changer
  c) pilot study

2 _____ says that you just can't do that.
  a) Paradigm shifting   **b)** Game-changing
  c) Conventional wisdom

3 Have you ever considered _____ one of those?
  a) to buy   **b)** buying   **c)** buy

4 I didn't manage _____ him last night.
  a) to call   **b)** calling   **c)** call

5 I think that we need _____ with a new plan.
  a) to come up   **b)** coming up   **c)** come up

6 I decided to do this job _____ a difference where it matters.
  a) to make   **b)** making   **c)** make

7 It's really strange to see you _____ that.
  a) to do   **b)** doing   **c)** do

8 We started out early this morning, with the aim _____ getting home at five.
  a) for   **b)** in   **c)** of

9 We have absolutely no hesitation _____ recommending him for the job.
  a) for   **b)** in   **c)** of

10 She's had a passion _____ art since we visited Florence.
  a) for   **b)** in   **c)** of

11 You really should think about the _____ of your actions.
  a) implications   **b)** consequences   **c)** motivations

12 When I lost my job I spent several weeks _____.
  a) vulnerable   **b)** destitute   **c)** on welfare

13 They are well-known for their _____ work in the community.
  a) altruistic   **b)** compassionate   **c)** philanthropic

14 The car _____ that stange sound all morning.
  a) is making   **b)** has been making
  c) will have been making

15 By this evening, he _____ for more than twelve hours.
  a) has been working   **b)** has worked
  c) will have been working

16 I was really shocked when I heard what she _____.
  a) had done   **b)** was doing
  c) will have been doing

17 The children _____ to visit next weekend.
  a) will have been hoping   **b)** will have hoped
  c) are hoping

18 They took their _____ to the bank to secure funding.
  a) business model   **b)** profit driven
  c) online transaction

19 I'm part of the _____ – I rent out my parking space.
  a) umbrella term   **b)** on-demand access
  c) access economy

20 Children who are _____ for good work usually do well.
  a) derided   **b)** engaged   **c)** praised

21 If you don't know the answer, make _____ guess.
  a) an educated   **b)** a perfectionist
  c) a highly beneficial

22 _____ they disagreed on a number of key issues.
  a) Provided that   **b)** It seems as if   **c)** But for

23 _____, just ask someone else.
  a) If in doubt   **b)** If so   **c)** If any

24 She doesn't fit in. She's a _____ out of water.
  a) chip   **b)** fish   **c)** cloud

25 Your great idea is unfortunately coming apart at the _____.
  a) arms   **b)** shoulders   **c)** seams

26 I really wish they would _____ the initiative in class.
  a) find   **b)** take   **c)** offer

27 We can talk about _____ you want, OK?
  a) whenever   **b)** whichever   **c)** whatever

28 This really isn't _____ I imagined life would be.
  a) where   **b)** when   **c)** how

29 You can't just rely on _____ to get the correct answer.
  a) intellect   **b)** intuition   **c)** fertile imagination

30 It was just a _____ decision to study music, nothing else.
  a) versatile   **b)** tried and tested
  c) spur of the moment

RESULT   /30

VOCABULARY

JOB HUNTING

1 Add letters to complete the phrases in the sentences.

1 There have been a number of applicants for the job but none s_ _ _ _ o_ _ _.

2 What we're looking for are people who can c_ _ _ _ _ _ ideas clearly.

3 One major drawback with this industry is the profusion of b_ _ _ _ _ _ _ _ _.

4 I'd consider deleting your Facbook account; your d_ _ _ _ _ _ _ f_ _ _ _ _ _ _ _ could put off potential employers.

5 Given the emphasis on online marketing, this role requires d_ _ _ _ _ _ _ l_ _ _ _ _ _ _ to be of the highest level.

6 Wearing the 'wrong' clothing to an interview can still j_ _ _ _ _ _ _ _ _ _ your chances.

7 She's a phenomenal communicator, with some of the best s_ _ _ _ s_ _ _ _ _ I've seen.

8 I'd appreciate any advice you could give me. I'm a complete n_ _ _ _ _ _.

9 I think he'd be an interesting proposition; he's got a good t_ _ _ _ _ r_ _ _ _ _.

10 Remember, when you get into the interview p_ _ _ _ u_ _ your strengths wherever possible.

READING

2 A Read the article and choose the best description. The article is

a) a light-hearted description of the process of job hunting.

b) an irreverent observation of the process of job interviews.

c) a serious overview of the challenges facing job-seekers.

AND HOW DID YOU HEAR ABOUT THIS JOB?

Home   News   Reviews   Listings   **Advice**   Sign out   Register

So, it's the big day. The seemingly interminable trawl through online ads has come to an end. Your CV has passed muster, picked from a teetering pile. The cursory email invite responded to in just the right manner – a curious, enthusiastic yet <u>placatory</u> tone. And now? The interview.

Despite recent attempts to revolutionise the concept – such as candidates interviewing one another – the job interview has remained predominantly unchanged. A formalised rite of passage for those embarking on their first steps into the world of work. A familiar, albeit terrifying, opportunity for reinvention when changing employer or role. It's perhaps that sense of familiarity which has kept things consistent. There's no need to change a long-running format if everybody knows how things work. But, occasionally, familiarity does breed contempt. Clichéd questions can be hard enough to answer sincerely once, so what do you do when you're on your second or even third interview? Well, one option is to think about what the interviewer really wants to know.

We've probably all heard the ice-breaker, 'Tell me a little about yourself.' This short phrase can <u>instil</u> panic in even the most battle-hardened interviewee. Perhaps they won't like the real me? Perhaps I should have checked my digital footprint for compromising posts? But remember, it's not really a question at all. Employers are sometimes looking to see what motivates you to succeed in your personal life, but on the whole, they are just trying to reduce tension. Keep it simple, and wherever possible avoid <u>rambling</u> anecdotes.

Then the real questions begin, 'What attracted you to this position?' Shorthand for 'Are you sure what this job <u>entails</u>, and can you see yourself doing it for the foreseeable future?' The key here is be enthusiastic and get specific. Think about an aspect of the job that genuinely interests you, and be prepared to discuss it in detail. Show the interviewer you've thought things through. Some sage advice is not to describe how the advertised position is exactly what you're doing right now only to then say how much you dislike your current job.

Next we get to the dreaded territory of career aspirations: 'Where do you see yourself in five years?' For an employer, it's all about ascertaining your sense of drive and expectation. They want you to show some vision beyond the next pay day and demonstrate a realistic understanding of career progression within their industry. We live in an era where people may have multiple, often overlapping careers, differing from the traditional 'a job for life' idea, but you should be able to clearly demonstrate your aspirations. Experiences <u>augment</u> others, and these will build a more individualised career path. When asked this question, think about which opportunities are available. And be honest about how you want to approach them.

Honesty and self-awareness are also key for that classic question 'Can you tell me about a recent failure?' What the employer is seeking here is evidence of an ability to learn from lessons, to critically assess and evaluate past experiences. Too often they get a litany of woes that stray into admissions of <u>incompetence</u>. Or, perhaps worse, a sense of denial. While you want to appear confident, pretending that you've never made mistakes can damage your chances.

Remember, interviewers aren't looking for a perfect person; they are looking for someone who fits.

B Read the article again. Are the statements true (T), false (F) or not given (NG)?

1 The writer thinks that the majority of people would be satisfied if traditional approaches to job interviews were abandoned.
2 The writer believes that having substantial experience of job interviews puts you in a better position when you are asked tried and tested questions.
3 Even candidates who have considerable interview experience may often be concerned by questions that have a more personal tone.
4 When asked about oneself, it's useful to draw on detailed personal experiences to convey your character.
5 Employers may often be wary of candidates who compare current and prospective jobs.
6 Interviewers ask about aspirations to ensure that candidates have a clear vision of where they could end up within a business.
7 The writer believes that the notion of a long-term career path is a positive one.
8 Interviewers are likely to be attracted to candidates who cannot draw on an example of failure, as this shows they are well-adjusted.

C Complete the sentences with the underlined words in the article.

1 Stories of _____ and corruption within the firm are rife. It's only time before they're closed down.
2 It's not the first time they've had to _____ staff numbers with temporary consultants.
3 People sometimes assume that this role is fairly straightforward, but it _____ a lot more than you may think.
4 After our first conversation I was furious, but he was more _____ the next time we discussed things.
5 It's important to _____ a winning attitude in your staff if you want them to work effectively.
6 The CEO's speech was a _____ monologue on inspiration and motivation. Sadly, it achieved neither.

GRAMMAR
EXPRESSING MODALITY

3 Underline the correct alternative to complete the sentences.

1 **A:** Was that Tom I just saw in the lift?
   B: No, *it shouldn't have/it couldn't have* been. He's overseas on business.
2 **A:** I didn't say I'd have the report finished by tonight!
   B: Really? You *must/would* have forgotten your promise already!
3 **A:** Do you think it'll take long to employ a new boss?
   B: Probably. I *could/would* guess there'll be a fair number of applicants.
4 **A:** I'll phone Andy and ask what he thinks.
   B: You *should/had* better not ring now. It's far too late.
5 **A:** Look at that. There's plenty of food in the fridge.
   B: Oh. We *mustn't/needn't* have ordered pizza. Shall I cancel?
6 **A:** Aren't you coming to the film then?
   B: I'm sorry, I've got loads to do. You *should/could* go though. You'll like it.
7 **A:** Anyone interesting called?
   B: Let's see. Another sales call.
   A: I *might/must* have guessed. We're getting so many these days.
8 **A:** Where are they? Are they lost?
   B: Not sure, they *ought to/need to* be here by now.

4 Complete the article with the phrases in the box. Sometimes more than one answer is possible.

absolutely essential that	being able to	be capable of
could be that	may well	supposed to have
will undoubtedly	would guess	

Starting a new job is one of those rites of passage that invariably fills us with dread. You've overthrown any lingering anxieties, aced the interview and surpassed yourself in the seemingly unsympathetic face of HR. Now, it's ¹_____ you make it through the first day without causing a diplomatic incident, or at the least avoiding the mantle of office pariah. But wait a minute. Remember that while most new starters are ²_____ a modicum of talent, they ³_____ commit a number of mistakes as they get to grips with the buzzwords and acronyms that plague the modern workplace. You ⁴_____ need a few days just to decode what marketing mean by all that blue-sky thinking. And ⁵_____ tell your SAP from your elbow is a skill that takes time. If you're lucky, it ⁶_____ your workplace provides a mentoring system. While the cynical may say that you needn't depend upon the guidance of an office elder, remember, they are a vital resource. Under their tutelage you'll soon ⁷_____ navigating the pitfalls of open-plan office life, work the coffee machine and keep admin happy. And that, I ⁸_____, is all that most people want from a job.

WRITING

A COVER EMAIL; LEARN TO IMPROVE USE OF FORMAL LANGUAGE

5 A Complete the cover email with the phrases in the box.

> am accustomed to working under pressure
> am dedicated to the profession
> has an excellent reputation in
> has taught me to adapt to
> have extensive experience working with
> would be grateful for the opportunity to

To:

I am writing to apply for the position of content developer advertised on your company website. ªI was really happy to hear about this opening as Inov88 ¹_____ the profession. I've also been very impressed with your recent sales campaign and your move towards incorporating consumer-generated content into your marketing narrative.

I'd like to take this opportunity to draw attention to relevant aspects of my background:

- Since 2016 ᵇI have done lots of stuff like yours, developing online materials in a freelance capacity for a range of startups.
- This ²_____ working to a tight brief, while offering technical insights.
- I ³_____ a full range of current coding and design packages.
- My art school background provides an aesthetic understanding of design.

As my referees will attest, I ⁴_____ and to short deadlines that are commonplace within the industry. I am a team player with excellent communication skills and a desire to learn. Furthermore, I ⁵_____ and see myself working long-term with the right company. I consider Inov88 to be an ideal working environment to develop the skills and strategies which I currently possess. As a content developer with a vision for blending functionality and design, I believe I would be ᶜa definite plus for your company.

As requested, please find my CV attached. This includes contact information for three references, and a link to my online portfolio.

I ⁶_____ discuss my application in more detail, and to ᵈchat about how good I am. ᵉCall me at your convenience, and thank you for your ᶠcareful thoughts.

B Replace the underlined phrases in the email with the more formal phrases in the box.

> a real asset to   consideration
> explore my suitability for the position
> I have been involved in projects similar to
> I was particularly excited to discover
> Please contact me

C Read the job adverts. Take notes on the job you want to apply for, and why.

ONLINE MARKETER FOR INNOVATIVE FASHION STARTUP

€35,000–40,000

This is a rare opportunity to take on an exciting role in our European marketing team. We're seeking enthusiastic and self-motivated individuals with a head for fashion and a creative drive. Work with us to build brand loyalty, and move our strategy onto a range of digital platforms.

You will need:

excellent IT skills   creativity   flexibility

Send us your CV and a covering letter to …

Travel guides required

GoForth is a leading provider of language services within the tourism sector. We are currently recruiting bilingual travel guides for a range of assignments in a number of interesting and exotic locations. Your primary responsibility will be providing face-to-face interpreting, working alongside our local guides. The work is based throughout Asia and South America, so willingness to travel is a must.

Skills:
fluent English plus one other language
excellent communication skills
good organisational skills
ability to work with a variety of people and ability to improvise

Contact us on …

D Write a cover email of your own (250 words). Use some of the ideas from this unit to help you.

VOCABULARY

HONESTY

1 For 1–6, complete the second sentence so it has a similar meaning to the first. Use no more than five words and the word given.

1 I think it's about time that they owned up to the situation before things escalate. CLEAN
They _____ the situation before it escalates any further.

2 He's finally let everyone see how he really feels about things. TRUE
He's _____ at last.

3 She was spotted taking the money, so she's bound to get fired. RED
They _____, so I'm sure they'll fire her.

4 When it came out that her CV was fake, she was totally humiliated. FACE
She _____ the revelation that her CV was fake.

5 The documentary went some way to telling things exactly as they were. PICTURE
It _____ the circumstances to some extent.

6 I don't know why nobody wants to talk about this. It's important. OVER
Why is _____ such an important issue?

LISTENING

2 A Is it popular for students to get work experience where you're from? Note down some of the reasons why they might do it.

B ▶ 3.1 You are going to hear five short extracts where students talk about their work experience. Listen and write the reason why they chose the job (A–G) next to the speaker and question number (1–5). There are two options you don't need.

C Listen again. For questions 6–10 write next to each speaker (1–5) what benefits (A–G) they got from doing the job. There are two options you don't need.

A a tutor's recommendation		
B the international nature of the company	Speaker 1	1
C the opportunity to work on a cutting-edge project	Speaker 2	2
D convenience	Speaker 3	3
E the company's philosophy	Speaker 4	4
F the opportunity to extend their academic interests	Speaker 5	5
G the opportunity to work with animals		

A a greater sense of confidence		
B a better understanding of responsibility	Speaker 1	6
C new social opportunities	Speaker 2	7
D the chance to make new contacts	Speaker 3	8
E the chance to explore a new field	Speaker 4	9
F a clearer idea of future job plans	Speaker 5	10
G the chance to put ideas into practice		

D Match the underlined words and phrases from the recording with the definitions a)–f). Read the audio script on page 65 to help you.

1 … 'internship' is often just a <u>euphemism</u> for office dogsbody.

2 I'm not <u>averse</u> to hard work …

3 I need as much as I can just to <u>keep afloat</u>, living here.

4 … some of the <u>nuances</u> of different working cultures.

5 … want to be at the <u>forefront</u> of change.

6 I'd been studying abroad on an exchange when this <u>cropped up</u>.

a) to stay financially stable
b) having a strong dislike of something
c) the leading or most important position or place
d) substituting an offensive word or phrase for something less offensive
e) a subtle difference in or shade of meaning
f) occur or come to one's notice unexpectedly

GRAMMAR

PASSIVES

3 Rewrite each sentence in the passive. Do not use the underlined words.

1 <u>You</u> have to complete a membership form.

_____

2 <u>They</u> don't know what happened to the plane.

_____

3 <u>They</u> expect <u>her</u> to make a full recovery.

_____

4 <u>The photographers</u> take photographs after the event.

_____

5 <u>They</u> stopped <u>playing</u> the match after an hour.

_____

6 It's time <u>the authorities</u> did something about climate change.

_____

7 <u>Officials</u> have announced that Los Angeles is to host the next games.

_____

8 <u>Nobody</u> has heard from the climbers since last Friday.

_____

4 For 1–7, complete the second sentence so it has a similar meaning to the first. Use no more than five words and the word given.

1 It was very easy for someone to steal the money because you left it out. STOLEN
You left the money out which explains
_____ easily.

2 Careful with my laptop! You could break it! HAVE
My laptop _____ – be more careful!

3 Journalists have estimated that his transfer is worth at least €80 million to the club. ESTIMATED
His transfer _____ somewhere in the region of €80 million.

4 They regarded him so highly that they forgave his occasional outbursts. HELD
He _____, so they forgave his occasional outbursts.

5 She was apparently given the wrong information on the interview date. MISINFORMED
She seems _____ the interview date.

6 Your phone needs repairing. NEED
You _____ phone repaired.

7 We all decided to organise a fundraising event next March. WOULD
It _____ all organise a fundraising event the following March.

VOCABULARY *PLUS*

METAPHORS

5 Circle the correct options to complete the text.

One current business trend enjoying an element of success is the pop-up shop. There have been a whole host of these sprouting ¹_____ in the most unlikely of locations. We've had trendy barbers, cereal cafés and artisan bakeries in places such as abandoned schools or derelict stations. Not all of them have been able to keep their heads ²_____ water, but on the whole, the novel approach to product and premises has borne ³_____. There has been one particularly ⁴_____ issue to contend with, though. And that's gentrification. The young, predominatly well-off owners of these establishments may well be reaping the ⁵_____ of their enterprise, but just how much of their revenue is trickling ⁶_____ to the communites where they've set up shop? Critics would say they are just taking up spaces and places that could better serve the community, and that local residents are being priced out by upmarket incomers. While it's unfeasible to suggest pop-ups plough ⁷_____ hard-earned profits into urban renewal, it could be argued that more could be done to ensure grass-⁸_____ support. Hiring a few local people might stem the ⁹_____ of criticism. As would occasionally offering something that your neighbours might be interested in purchasing. Call me a ¹⁰_____ blanket, but I can't really see many people round here blowing the best part of a day's wage on a burger. Even if it is hand-ground beef served in a pumpkin seed artisan brioche. With quinoa fries …

1 **a)** on	**b)** through	**c)** up
2 **a)** around	**b)** above	**c)** over
3 **a)** fruit	**b)** branch	**c)** leaf
4 **a)** prickly	**b)** thorny	**c)** spiky
5 **a)** gains	**b)** prizes	**c)** rewards
6 **a)** through	**b)** down	**c)** along
7 **a)** back	**b)** on	**c)** in
8 **a)** leaves	**b)** green	**c)** roots
9 **a)** flow	**b)** flood	**c)** stream
10 **a)** damp	**b)** wet	**c)** moist

VOCABULARY

POLITICAL COLLOCATIONS

1 A Complete the texts with the words in the box.

| allocate | bridge | enforce | set |
| promote | shape | stand up | tackle |

A

Personally, I'm getting more and more dispirited with the state of things. It's about time that this government showed that it's willing to ¹_____ for the rights of public sector workers. The service that they provide the country is invaluable, but they are constantly being affected by growing workloads and pay freezes. So many politicians say that they want to ²_____ the gap between the public and private sector, but there's been little change.

B

What changes would I like to see? Well, our infrastructure is lagging far behind what you'd expect, compared to a lot of other countries. I'd like to see the government ³_____ resources to improved telecommunications. Things might be good in larger urban areas, but businesses elsewhere are beset with all kinds of issues. Poor broadband connectivity jeopardises any chance of competing on a level playing field. They need to ⁴_____ a realistic budget, and invest in fibre optic networks throughout the country. You can't ⁵_____ the development of a digital economy if access is restricted.

C

Can you really trust them to change anything? They constantly promise to ⁶_____ corruption and then you find out that they've been misappropriating funds themselves. If they want to restore people's faith in the political process, they need to be much more open, and proactive. Take tax evasion, for example. Why can't the government just ⁷_____ regulations and make sure that multinationals pay their fair share? What we really need is a real sense of leadership. Politicians should be the ones to ⁸_____ policy.

B Do you agree with any of the views expressed above? Why/Why not?

FUNCTION

EVADING A QUESTION

2 A Complete the interview with the phrases in the box.

| all I'm saying is that there's a problem |
| let me just add to what I was saying   let me put it into perspective |
| that quote was taken out of context   what we have to take into account |

A: So, Minister, according to the front page of today's papers, you claimed, 'Students get more than their fair share of government funds.' Would you care to elaborate on that?

B: Well, before we begin, I'd like to say ¹_____. I'm a firm supporter of extending free tuition where possible.

A: So, can you explain your party's plans to cut bursaries for students from low-income backgrounds?

B: Well, ²_____ is that there are many reasons for reassessing the education budget. Especially with regards to tertiary education.

A: Do you feel that perhaps they are unworthy of your investment?

B: Before I answer that, ³_____. The state of the public finances left by the last government has meant we have to look across the board at spending decisions.

A: So, you've not got enough money?

B: Listen, ⁴_____ with continuing some of the policies that we inherited. However, we're committed to providing affordable solutions.

A: By reducing education spending and allowing tuition fees to go uncapped?

B: OK, ⁵_____. There are many other countries where this is happening. We need a more competitive model.

B ▷ 3.2 Listen and check.

LEARN TO

CONTROL THE AGENDA

3 Write responses with the prompts and your own words.

1 There's really no need for new legislation to address the gender pay-gap.
due / all / with / respect

_____

2 As far as I'm concerned, climate change isn't really a key issue.
excuse / but / me / interrupting / for

_____

3 Economic success depends on encouraging big business. Their tax status is unimportant.
blunt / but / wish / I / be / don't / to

_____

4 Under our government, the homeless have more access to healthcare.
not / point / surely / but / that's / the

_____

5 Students shouldn't expect any more handouts from us.
saying / what / is / that / so / you're

_____

VOCABULARY

INFLUENCE

1 Match the sentence halves.

1 While she's not always right, her opinions tend to carry

2 Try to be a bit more assertive; I've noticed you give

3 I would prefer it if they didn't try to influence events

4 If I were you, I'd try not to put her

5 I find it amazing that so many people idolise

6 Athletes need to realise that they are important role

7 As far as I'm aware, her mother pulled

8 Perhaps one way to get on in this industry is to emulate

9 Looking back, I'd say that my judo coach was highly

10 As a child she always tended to be swayed

11 Her father was a talented musician, so she wanted to follow

12 He's overcome a number of early setbacks and become an

a) from behind the scenes. I'd rather succeed or fail on my own terms.

b) a lot of strings to get her the internship at the gallery.

c) by the views of her older siblings.

d) the best – if you aim high, you should achieve your goals.

e) inspiration to urban youth.

f) models and ensure that they behave accordingly.

g) on a pedestal. She's got her failings, just like anyone else.

h) influential in terms of shaping my approach to self-discipline.

i) way to some of the more outspoken students in class.

j) a lot of weight with me.

k) celebrities who don't seem to have much going for them.

l) in his footsteps.

LISTENING

2 A Which of the photos do you think represents a good role model? Why?

B ▶ 4.1 Listen to a talk about the importance of role models. Complete the sentences with the exact word or short phrase you hear.

1 The speaker explains that due to our social nature we often modify behaviour by following peers with little recourse to _____.

2 She says that according to _____, having positive role models is an integral part of childhood development.

3 She explains that with repeated emulation and approval, role modelling can create _____.

4 In the past, a _____ or _____ was often perceived as an inspirational role model.

5 Research indicates that there is a benefit to observing _____ as well as others who are more inspirational.

6 We may be drawn to contrast rather than compare our behaviour with others when we are strongly affected by the _____.

7 Recent studies show that _____ benefits from having role models in close proximity.

8 According to neurobiologists, the learning triggered by mirror neurons aids _____ or _____.

C Match the underlined words and phrases from the recording with the definitions a)–f). Read the audio script on page 66 to help you.

1 … <u>subscribing</u> to similar mindsets is a fundamental part of our everyday lives.

2 In their most <u>nascent</u> form, role models are our parents and close family.

3 … online media <u>thrives</u> on the fascination for constant updates of celebrity achievement …

4 According to <u>cutting-edge</u> neurobiological studies …

5 Then doping scandals toppled our idols and <u>tarnished</u> both reputations and medals.

6 … having role models who are within your close environment may be more <u>efficacious</u> than those held in high regard …

a) coming into existence or beginning to display signs of future potential

b) ruin, make less valued or respected

c) innovative, leading the way

d) successful in producing a desired or intended result

e) expressing or agreeing with a proposal or idea

f) grow stronger, prosper or gain from

GRAMMAR
PARTICIPLE CLAUSES

3 Underline the correct alternatives. In two cases both alternatives are correct.

¹*Injured/Having been injured* at a relatively early stage in his playing career, Brian Clough went on to become one of the most influential figures in European football. ²*Having had/Having* his opportunities for glory on the field cut short, he was tireless in his pursuit as a coach and manager. ³*Confronted/Confronting* with any injustice committed by club owners, he would support his playing staff principles like no one else. And this ensured that his teams were loyal and committed. Clough was also a strong disciplinarian and with a few cutting words could have a grown man ⁴*shaken/shaking* with fear. But overall, he was a dreamer and a doer who disregarded conventions, ⁵*determined/having determined* to achieve whatever he set out to do.
As manager at Nottingham Forest in the late 1970s, Clough was ⁶*obsessed/obsessing* with showing the world that a small club could contend on the greatest stage. In 1979, he had his chance. ⁷*Having beaten/Beating* more experienced rivals on the way, his team played in the prestigious European Cup Final – and won. ⁸*Considered/Considering* how difficult it was to retain a European title, many thought that victory was a one-off. Yet a year later, Clough triumphed again.

4 Rewrite the sentences using a participle clause.

1 The fans roared and cheered as they celebrated her victory.
_____

2 She acquired the family business as a teenager, so was reluctant to sell.
_____

3 They were reprimanded by the authorities, then asked to leave the country.
_____

4 When I considered all the options, I decided not to apply for the job.
_____

5 They realised that there was nobody in, so they left a message with a neighbour.
_____

6 If you look after it carefully, this watch could last you a lifetime.
_____

7 The portrait, which was painted sixty years ago, depicts my grandmother.
_____

8 Kate and Max had a huge argument and then left without saying anything.
_____

VOCABULARY *PLUS*
THREE-PART MULTI-WORD VERBS

5 Complete the text with the correct prepositions.

There comes a point in most people's lives when they need to face ¹_____ to the fact that they may never win an Olympic medal, write a *New York Times* bestseller, or appear on Broadway. Yet while some achievements may spectacularly fail to live up ²_____ expectations, it is important that we set ourselves goals and acknowledge that coming up ³_____ adversity is all part of the process. According to psychologists, too often people back ⁴_____ of challenging situations instead of committing to effort. It's worth considering how this impacts on the people around you. Evidently, while children often seem to look up ⁵_____ sportstars and celebrities as role models, they are more likely to find a close relative or family member to be a compelling source of inspiration. While many of us might not feel ⁶_____ to being put on a pedestal, we should try to take time to ascertain what others get ⁷_____ of watching us try to fulfil our goals. Next time you fall short of your aims, try to hold ⁸_____ on being overtly critical of yourself. If you can, come up ⁹_____ a way of reframing your failure as part of the learning process. This positive spin is a worthwhile lesson to pass on to anyone, which more than makes up ¹⁰_____ not achieving quite what you wanted. You'll become the kind of person that people want to emulate, and a better role model for that.

6 Complete the sentences with the correct form of a multi-word verb from Exercise 5.

1 If you're not keen on the training course, it's still not too late to _____ going.

2 I can't believe he _____ that singer – he's not exactly a positive role model.

3 They did everything they could to _____ attending the meeting, but in the end they had to make an appearance.

4 His older brother graduated with a first from Oxford, so he's got a lot to _____.

5 They _____ a number of complaints from local residents during the planning process.

6 I _____ an ingenious plan of how to pass the test without doing much revision.

7 Sorry, we don't really _____ doing much this weekend. Can we reschedule our meeting?

8 It's about time that you _____ the fact that nobody is going to do the work for you.

9 I realise it's important, but can we _____ making a decision until later?

10 What a beautiful evening. It certainly _____ the lousy weather this afternoon.

VOCABULARY

SOCIAL MEDIA

1 Underline the correct alternative to complete the sentences.

1 When you log on to an aggregated newsfeed, you can tell that a certain amount of *trolling/filtering* is going on, as some events just don't get sufficient coverage.

2 A great number of chat rooms are perceived by the mainstream media as being *algorithms/echo chambers* for increasingly extreme viewpoints.

3 Self-selecting discussion groups make it easier to have your views *reinforced/faked* by like-minded individuals.

4 The list of most popular stories is generated by an *algorithm/screenshot*, so you can't really expect it to reflect anything like an objective news agenda.

5 One of the biggest dangers in this *post-truth/fake* era is that any voice of dissent can easily be disregarded as lacking credibility.

6 Moderators frequently accuse critics of *hacking/trolling*, which is often enough to ensure that they are removed from a discussion entirely.

READING

2 A Read the blog post about the role of algorithms and technology in the media. Do you agree with any of the views given?

B Which person gives each of these opinions about technology and media?

1 Current trends towards filtered news are worrying.

2 It's too simplistic to be unquestionably critical of technology in the media.

3 Much current online media content is frivolous.

4 Technology is important in terms of generating content, as well as selecting it.

5 Believing that social media is a trustworthy source of news is misguided.

6 Being exposed to a broad range of narratives and perspectives is vital.

7 Traditional journalism and technology can coexist to the benefit of the former.

8 The best way to address fake news is to become a more critical reader.

Machines making the media

Last week, we asked readers to comment on some of the key issues actively affecting the fourth estate. Digital journalism is undergoing a huge transformation – from the economics of online distribution to far-ranging questions over editorial impartiality. Fake news, post-truths and content as click-bait are all concerns that our readers have with established news outlets. On top of this, voices of discontent seem to be clamouring when it comes to the burgeoning influence of citizen journalists and bloggers on mainstream media titles. Here's a snapshot of your opinions:

Alexa, San Francisco

The most disconcerting aspect for me has to be the amount of trust that readers place in news feeds from social media. It's worrying that anyone would begin to contemplate these as an oracle of the truth to begin with, but when I started to analyse retweets and promoted content, I was aghast. You cannot underestimate the potential damage that blind obedience to an algorithm is going to wreak. Artificial Intelligence  constantly gets outsmarted by hoaxers and those with insalubrious agendas. But to blame the technology outright seems a bit infantile. People really need to learn to evaluate content better – and to cross reference stories. A bit of rudimentary fact-checking is essential when reading any content.

Paul, Rome

I've heard the arguments that readers are becoming overwhelmed by the huge quantities of information and misinformation washing around social media, but I'm not won over. There are products out there where you can quite rigorously set your own filters, and personalise news so it's relevant to you. Now, in principle that sounds like a good thing, as I could avoid scrolling through screeds of lurid stories about z-grade celebs. But won't I just end up in some content rich echo chamber? I think diversity of news sources is important. There might be a story that piques my interest, which I wouldn't have necessarily been immediately drawn to. I'd hate to think that I was actively limiting my horizons as a consumer of news.

Sarah, Melbourne

Oh, we all hate algorithms, right? It's those mendacious machines trying to overpower our free press and promote post-truths. Wouldn't the world of journalism be better without technology? Er, no. I think a number of your readers would be intrigued to learn just how much of the online content that they read has been written by an algorithm. They  aren't just curating content from blogs and media backwaters. They are writing the stuff, too. And I for one think that's laudable. More outlets are using algorithms to write reports with predictable formulae, and that frees up 'real' journalists to do something a bit more investigative.

GRAMMAR

INTRODUCTORY *IT* AND *THERE*

3 Underline the correct alternative to complete the sentences.

1 *It's/There's* a lot to be said for getting someone to pull a few strings now and again.

2 *It's/There's* generally believed that you're more likely to be successful if you've had positive role models from an early age.

3 Do you think *it's/there's* any chance that there could have been some kind of mistake?

4 *It/There* pains me to say it, but I'm not convinced of his innocence at all.

5 *It/There* appears to be a lot of confusion on social media regarding the authenticity of early reports.

6 *It's/There's* a pity you didn't get here sooner – I'm sure he would have loved to have met you.

7 *It's/There's* no coincidence that so few graduates are applying to become teachers.

8 *It/There* must be some reason why you've been avoiding me lately.

9 *It's/There's* a mistake to think we've seen the last of fake news in politics.

10 *It's/There's* shocking how little was known about the issue online.

4 For 1–8, complete the second sentence so it has a similar meaning to the first. Use the words given.

1 Everyone knows the website is full of fake news.
common / knowledge

_____

2 It looks like there's been an accident up ahead.
there / seem

_____

3 There'll be a huge controversy when the story gets out.
there / sure

_____

4 The choice of film is entirely yours.
it / up / watch

_____

5 I only just realised what she meant.
it / dawned

_____

6 You should have been at the show – you would have loved it.
it / pity / missed

_____

7 People are optimistic that the conflict is coming to an end.
it / hoped

_____

8 We shouldn't discuss the matter again.
there / little / point

_____

WRITING

A REPORT; LEARN TO USE USEFUL PHRASES

5 A Read the email request for reports. Then make two columns in a notebook. Put the ideas for positive and negative effects in the box below under each heading.

To		From	

In line with a change of policy, the college is proposing a stop in supplying print newspapers in the student common room. Any students wishing to read news stories can do so online. Please write a report about the positive and negative effects of this proposal to the governing council, which supervises student life on campus. Include recommendations as to how to minimise any negative effects. We need about 280–320 words.

Positive effects	Negative effects

advertising   environmental impact
breadth of titles / diversity of perspectives
issues with access
impact on opportunity to discuss articles socially
questions over accuracy of content
regularity of updates
immediate access to forums/blogs related to content

B Add any more ideas of your own for positive/negative effects.

C Write your report on the college's proposal. Include an introduction, the negative effects of the proposal, the positive effects and a conclusion.

VOCABULARY

PERSUASION

1 Complete the sentences with the words in the box.

compelling	credible	earnest	genuine
persuasive	pertinent	pushy	succinct

1 While their argument is _____ in parts, I need a bit more evidence until I'm thoroughly convinced.

2 She made a really _____ speech which resulted in the council offering renewed support for the project.

3 Although he made _____ assurances that things would change, sadly little has improved.

4 In a brief and _____ manner I let everyone know exactly what I thought of their ideas.

5 Given his ties with the car industry, I'm not sure any of his views on the environmental impact of diesel engines are that _____.

6 If you can't say anything _____, then there's little point you being involved in the discussion.

7 He seemed quite _____ when we met, but I've heard a lot to make me question whether I should trust him.

8 One thing I can't stand is _____ parents who seem to live vicariously through their kids.

---

new save edit   share

At its inception, the advertising industry tended to follow established sets of rules – [1]choice, cost and consumer benefit were key to an effective campaign. The range of products was limited, and therefore relatively easy to manage. [2]No longer is that model sufficient when it comes to selling to time-poor, choice-rich consumers. Over the last two decades, the advertising industry has undergone substantial changes. Brands are now seeking more novel ways to capture the public's consciousness. [3]Online advertising is a creative's playground, where opportunities to explore the medium are seemingly boundless.The goal is to maximise coverage, while minimising cost. [4]If you hit the right balance, you can win over a whole new customer-base. If you hit the headlines, you can go global in a matter of minutes. Ask most advertising teams how to create a successful campaign, and they will usually respond [5]'Make it memorable.' In the last few years, online advertisements have come into their own as a creative medium. Often a successful advert will be liked and retweeted more than news stories, and the form has become almost an art in and of itself. [6]So, who tends to respond to these ads? Market-based research shows that 16–25 year-olds are the most likely to refer social media friends to viral marketing campaigns. But there is also evidence that high-impact campaigns, such as extended ads that blend extreme sports footage with product placement, are popular too.

FUNCTION

PERSUASIVE TECHNIQUES IN PRESENTATIONS

2 A Read the extract below left from a presentation about advertising. Match the underlined examples with the persuasive techniques a)–f).

a) direct speech   d) repetition

b) simile or metaphor   e) rhetorical question

c) negative inversion   f) the rule of 3

B Put the words in the correct order to make sentences.

1 only / is / the car / not / economical / stylish / it's / too
(negative inversion)

_____

2 wouldn't / who / deal / want / a / that / like?
(rhetorical question)

_____

3 pressure / under / cool / stay / collected / and / calm
(the rule of 3)

_____

4 successful / need / work / to / be / you / harder / play / to / hard / and
(repetition)

_____

5 'love / team / being / we / part / join / the / of / us'
(direct speech)

_____

6 dog / world / dog / eat / here / It's / a
(metaphor)

_____

C ▶ 4.2 Listen and check.

LEARN TO

USE ADJECTIVE ALLITERATION

3 A Complete the sentences with the missing word.

1 Despite the obvious pressures, he's a great presenter; he's self-confident, successful and s_ _ _ _ _ _ _t.

2 I found him generous and g_ _ _ _ _e although a little juvenile in character.

3 She's incredibly patient and pertinent without being overly p_ _ _ _ _ _ _ _ _e. That's a good thing.

4 I liked what they had to say; they were confident, c_ _ _ _ _ _ _ _ _g and concise.

5 The information we received was both critical and c_ _ _ _ _ _e.

6 I'm not overly fond of your boss; he's proud, p_ _ _y and pompous.

7 What a lovely old bloke – articulate, urbane and e_ _ _ _ _t.

B ▶ 4.3 Listen and check.

GRAMMAR   EXPRESSING MODALITY

1 Underline the correct alternatives.

1 Being able *at/to* multitask is so important in the modern workplace.

2 It's *an absolute/absolutely* essential that they take the time to find the right person.

3 It *could/would* be that we see some big changes round here pretty soon.

4 When you get there, they *may/shall* well ask you for some ID.

5 I *should/would* guess that you've never eaten it before, have you?

6 You *needn't/wouldn't* have brought me flowers, thank you.

7 He *can't/mustn't* have forgotten our arrangement. We said be here at seven.

8 Come on, we're *supposed/supposing* to have left half an hour ago.

9 Do you think that she'll be capable *at/of* speaking to us?

10 This discovery *shall/will* undoubtedly change the way we think about our ancestors.

VOCABULARY   REVIEW 1

2 Match the sentence halves.

1 I'm surprised she didn't get offered the job, as her track

2 If you want to win the electorate's trust back, you must come

3 I had hoped that this government would shape

4 It's really important that you remember to play

5 It'll take a long time to bridge the

6 Did you hear what happened? She was caught red-

7 There's a meeting next week where they allocate

8 It's about time that someone tackled

9 The fact that she speaks several languages is a strong

10 It was all rather embarrassing. He lost

a) corruption in that country. It's a disgrace.

b) resources to local councils.

c) gap, although attitudes to gender pay isssues are changing.

d) to your strengths during interviews.

e) handed taking money from the till.

f) policy in a more progressive fashion.

g) face when news of his company's situation came out.

h) record in the industry is better than most.

i) clean about what you did wrong.

j) selling point for potential employers.

GRAMMAR   PASSIVES

3 For 1–10, complete the second sentence so it has a similar meaning to the first. Use no more than five words and the correct form of the word given.

1 We decided to try applying for the grant again next year.
WOULD
It _____ apply for funding the following year.

2 Apparently the money was taken by an employee.
APPEARS
The money _____ by someone who works there.

3 Your laptop needs updating.
NEED
You _____ updated.

4 Experts have estimated that the fund is worth at least £5 million.
ESTIMATED
The fund _____ somewhere in the region of £5 million.

5 I don't have anything else to add to this discussion.
SAID
There's nothing _____ the matter.

6 Careful with your phone. It could get stolen.
HAVE
Your phone _____ – be more careful!

7 I hope that they don't want to film the interview this time.
WON'T
I'm hoping the interview _____ on this occasion.

8 Rumour has it the couple are planning a divorce.
THOUGHT
The couple _____ planning a divorce.

9 Their team beat ours in the semi-finals.
GOT
We _____ them in the semi-finals.

10 We have agreed to talk things through next week.
WILL
It has _____ discuss the matter later.

VOCABULARY PLUS METAPHORS

4 Underline the correct alternatives.

1 Although he's not a great statesman, he has incredible grass *branch/roots* support.
2 She's been *blossoming/reaping* the rewards of a successful TV debut.
3 Don't mention work. It's a bit of a *thorny/spiky* issue at the moment.
4 There are so many new businesses sprouting *out/up* in the neighbourhood.
5 We sat in the kitchen and he *flooded/poured* out all his sorrows.
6 You really need to *branch/leaf* out a bit more and see other people.
7 My protests were drowned *out/in* by their raucous laughter.
8 There's been a lot of compromise. We had to *water down/pour out* our ideas.

FUNCTION EVADING A QUESTION

5 Complete the answers to the questions with the phrases in the box.

> add to what I was saying   brought that up
> needs addressing   put it into perspective
> saying is there's a problem   take into account
> taken out of context

1 **A:** Is it true that you claimed people should continue working until seventy-five?
  B: Well, before I start, that quote was _____.

2 **A:** But you do feel that the ageing workforce is an issue for concern?
  B: It's definitely a point that _____ by society in general.

3 **A:** Would you say your government has done enough about it?
  B: Listen, all I'm _____ that we all need to resolve.

4 **A:** Why is the issue so pressing now, though? What's gone wrong?
  B: Well, you need to _____ demographics, the business view …

5 **A:** So, have these demands been made by business leaders?
  B: Well, I'm glad you _____. There have been lots of supportive voices.

6 **A:** Are they putting pressure on you to change current policy?
  B: If I could _____, they are offering lots of good advice …

7 **A:** Don't you think this will be deeply unpopular with the electorate?
  B: Well, let me _____ – there are other places where this happens.

VOCABULARY REVIEW 2

6 Complete the text with the words in the box.

> compelling   credible   fake news   genuine
> idolise   persuasive   trolling   unbiased

These days I need a fairly [1]_____ reason to look at a newspaper – online or offline. It's a pretty sad state of affairs, but when there's a proliferation of [2]_____ clouding the picture it's pretty hard to put your faith in the fourth estate. However, as rolling news has become more ubiquitous, the need for material of [3]_____ importance has been displaced by the need for content. In the past, a journalist would take time to build a narrative, offer context, draw on a range of perspectives and sources. You can't write a [4]_____ piece, that'll genuinely engage readers, without it. My view is that now it's a less [5]_____ industry, especially as fact-checking seems to have gone out of the window. And it's increasingly difficult to find an [6]_____ and impartial editorial view. Another issue I have is that a lot of the press seem to [7]_____ celebrities these days and it sends out an odd message because few of them are particularly wholesome role models. And online, well, just look at some of the [8]_____ that goes on in below-the-line comments. Articles are just a platform for people to spout bile.

GRAMMAR PARTICIPLE CLAUSES

7 Rewrite the sentences, beginning with a participle clause.

1 Sarah left work early because she didn't feel well.
  _____

2 He had acquired a large sum of money through his own hard work, so was reluctant to pay tax on it.
  _____

3 Because she had started on the project, Ella was determined to complete it.
  _____

4 As we didn't want to offend him, we said nothing about his recent article.
  _____

5 As I haven't seen the film, I'm reticent to make a judgement.
  _____

6 The manager was impressed by Isa's work, so he extended her contract for a further six months.
  _____

7 She's a trained physiotherapist. She knows what effects that kind of exercise could have.
  _____

8 I don't speak Italian. I found life in Rome problematic.
  _____

VOCABULARY PLUS
THREE-PART MULTI-WORD VERBS

8 Complete 1–12 with a preposition to make a multi-word verb.

A Of course, you do have concerns when your kids start exploring the web on their own, but it's important to face ¹_____ to the fact that if you want them to be safe and effective online, they'll eventually have to come ²_____ with their own strategies. Trust plays an enormous role. I give them a certain amount of latitude and they promise not to get caught up ³_____ anything dodgy. It's not that I'm laid back, but I think the best way to show influence is to give them a sense of responsibility. Nine times out of ten it works. If they come ⁴_____ against anything they are unsure of, they'll talk it over with me. I prefer that than having to censor stuff.

B I initially got into blogging when I was at university. Without an editorial filter, you don't need to hold ⁵_____ on criticism. Although you have to make sure it's not libellous, obviously. I think it's important that people do engage with politics in a more constructive and critical way. I'd like it if people could look ⁶_____ to politicians again. Faith has been rocked a bit by scandals, and post-truth spin, but most people who get into politics actually do care. When you're in the public eye, there's a lot to live up ⁷_____ – but the challenge is worth it. I'm running for election this year. I suppose if I fail, I'll have my writing career to fall back ⁸_____.

C I really have no idea what people get out ⁹_____ doing this kind of thing day in, day out. I'm only taking part because my flatmate asked me, and I can't really back out ¹⁰_____ it now. I don't particularly feel ¹¹_____ to swimming in the river at the best of times, so why a gloomy November morning would appeal, I don't know. I suppose it is for a good cause, though. Once we're done here, I'm straight off for lunch with friends. Some hearty food and chat should make ¹²_____ for this nonsense.

GRAMMAR   INTRODUCTORY IT AND THERE

9 Correct the mistakes in the sentences.

1 It's a number of reasons how people doubt the authenticity of the story.
_____

2 It's harm in thinking things through.
_____

3 There's a mistake to make quick judgements about people.
_____

4 It's somewhere to say for considering different perspectives.
_____

5 There's not a coincidental that he began criticising the press when they attacked him.
_____

6 There's pity at your brother wasn't able to attend the party.
_____

7 There's you I has thanks for first introducing us.
_____

8 There worry me to seeing you like this.
_____

FUNCTION   PERSUASIVE TECHNIQUES IN PRESENTATIONS

10 Match the statements 1–6 with the persuasive techniques a)–f).

1 Don't miss hilarious comedian Jim Robbins at The Plaza: he's big, bold and brilliant!

2 Never have I seen such a successful team.

3 The ballet dancer seemed to float across the stage, as light as a feather.

4 What could be more difficult than that?

5 We spoke to our customers and they said, 'Give us more choice.'

6 This kind of product will be bought by every man, every woman, every child.

a) direct speech
b) simile or metaphor
c) negative inversion
d) repetition
e) rhetorical question
f) the rule of 3

CHECK

Circle the correct option to complete the sentences.

1 If you want to get noticed, you have to _____ your soft skills.
a) stand out   b) play up   c) convey

2 Late again! I _____ guessed there'd be a problem.
a) would have   b) should have   c) could have

3 I think you _____ interfere as you know nothing about the issue.
a) ought not to   b) ought to   c) ought

4 She _____ get the job after all. Let's just wait and see.
a) may well   b) will undoubtedly   c) might be able

5 It's time that they _____ about what they've been up to.
a) lost face   b) came clean   c) showed true colours

6 I suspect you might have _____ your role in their success.
a) given an accurate picture   b) glossed over
c) overstated

7 The milk _____ gone. Did you drink it all?
a) appeared to have been   b) appears to have
c) appears

8 Sorry, there is nothing more _____ about the matter.
a) said   b) being said   c) to be said

9 Don't be such a _____ blanket! Come to the party.
a) flood   b) water   c) wet

10 The council are hoping to plough _____ a lot of money into the community.
a) back   b) in   c) out

11 People are insisting they do something to _____ unemployment.
a) promote   b) tackle   c) shape

12 They could do more to _____ the gap between rich and poor.
a) enforce   b) set   c) bridge

13 He _____ have answered by now. I wonder where he is.
a) couldn't   b) ought   c) should

14 Her quote was completely taken _____ context.
a) into   b) out of   c) out from

15 That's an important issue that you've brought _____ for the agenda.
a) on   b) out   c) up

16 There's often someone diligently _____ behind the scenes.
a) pulling   b) swaying   c) working

17 She's an amazing _____ for disadvantaged kids. She does loads of charity work.
a) idol   b) role model   c) celebrity

18 _____ carefully, bonsai trees can last for years.
a) Looking after   b) Looked after   c) Look after

19 _____ the kids were sent to bed.
a) Kicked and screaming   b) Kicking and screaming
c) Kicking and scream

20 He's not really the kind of person that you'd look _____ to.
a) out   b) on   c) up

21 It amazes me what you get out _____ doing extreme sports.
a) of   b) on   c) from

22 Don't back _____ of our plans now, please.
a) in   b) out   c) up

23 Guess what? Someone _____ my email account.
a) hacked   b) faked   c) trolled

24 They've been accused of _____ stories they disagree with.
a) filtering   b) censoring   c) reinforcing

25 _____ seems like only yesterday we were in Moscow.
a) It   b) There   c) It's

26 _____ something to be said about homemade bread.
a) There   b) There's   c) It's

27 He gave a _____ and truly dramatic performance. It was mesmerising.
a) credible   b) pertinent   c) compelling

28 Well, I believe her. She's _____ in what she says.
a) earnest   b) pushy   c) succinct

29 _____ have you listened to me!
a) Never once   b) Not once   c) Not ever

30 If you fancy a change, these are cheap as _____.
a) chips   b) fries   c) potatoes

RESULT   /30

5)) BODY

LISTENING

1 A Which of the following do you think has the biggest impact on your general health? Why?

diet   exercise   genetics   stress

B ▶ 5.1 Listen to part of a discussion between two researchers talking about theories of what makes a body healthy. For questions 1–5, choose the best answer a), b), c) or d) according to what you hear.

1 What point does Charlotte de Witte make about general understanding of the microbiome?
   a) The importance of genetics is overstated.
   b) The definition of the concept has been oversimplified.
   c) It isn't as detailed as researchers would like.
   d) It requires increased investment before it will offer any answers.

2 When discussing the Human Microbiome Project, Luke Slater reveals
   a) his displeasure that the media had little interest in its findings.
   b) his frustration that its successes had only a momentary impact.
   c) his doubt that anyone will be interested in it long-term.
   d) his enthusiasm for the scope and breadth of resulting research.

3 What view is stated about emergent technology in the field?
   a) It is only useful when it has a defined role.
   b) It tends to fail on a regular basis.
   c) It provides ongoing detailed insights into investigation.
   d) It has a theoretical use but little else.

4 When discussing promoting microbiome health, both researchers agree that
   a) the public response is often depressing.
   b) people are well aware of the issues surrounding it.
   c) there is a need to fight public preconceptions.
   d) interest is generally higher among those who exercise regularly.

5 What final conclusion do the researchers reach about diet?
   a) Minimal changes to diet could positively affect the microbiome.
   b) Poor diet directly causes autoimmune and allergic diseases.
   c) The more fat you have, the more bacteria exist in your gut.
   d) The most successful and healthy diets are voluntary.

GRAMMAR

NOUN PHRASES

2 Complete the noun phrases using the correct form of the words in brackets and add any words where necessary.

1 The film is (late / series / adaptations / Marvel studios).
_____

2 I took part in (organise / class / focus / high impact / calorie / burn / exercise).
_____

3 He thinks it is a (rapid / change / market / offer / potential / massive / sales).
_____

4 This book is ideal for anyone (try / be / better / organise / and / seek / long-term / success).
_____

5 (Ground / break / experiment / research / conduct / Europe) proved the theory.
_____

6 She gave (series / talks / environment / protect / relevant / general public).
_____

3 Rewrite the sentences using a suitable noun phrase to replace the underlined phrase.

1 Theirs is an industry whose importance is increasing.
_____

2 She works for an organisation which is international but little known.
_____

3 To cook it really well, use one cup of rice to two cups of water in that ratio.
_____

4 I'd rather not go to classes that are organised – they don't suit the plans which I have for the long-term.
_____

5 His speeches are brilliant, but he often has opinions that are frustrating because they are ambiguous.
_____

6 Try to avoid products with sugars that are added, or salt contents that are high.
_____

7 I find that foodie forums online are one of the ways of learning about recipes that is best.
_____

8 Most of the issues that people in the article mentioned were completely irrelevant.
_____

9 Their fashion campaign which happened recently attracted criticism by members of the public.
_____

10 Having read your proposal, I think that's a solution which is practical and has a low impact on cost.
_____

VOCABULARY
COLLOCATIONS

4 Match words from boxes A and B to make collocations to complete the sentences. Use the correct form.

A

| achieve   deliver (x2)   discuss |
| enhance (x2)   trigger (x2)   sustain (x2) |

B

| a host of benefits   a memory |
| an aspect of   appearance   capacity |
| interest in   long-term motivation |
| rapid weight gain   success |
| tangible results |

1 A combination of a lack of exercise and poor diet was sufficient to _____ in the control group.

2 The renovation of the concert hall was intended to _____ to accommodate bigger events.

3 Looking at the photographs suddenly _____ of long-forgotten childhood holidays.

4 There are serious questions being asked about whether the policy will ever _____ promised to the electorate.

5 A gluten-free diet is supposed to _____ to anyone who has experienced food intolerances.

6 My problem is that I'm so capricious. I can barely _____ one activity before growing tired of it.

7 Could we _____ your study which I disagree with? Your findings on weight loss seem inconclusive.

8 It's doubtful that she'll _____ to continue with her training after the marathon. Her results aren't satisfactory.

9 _____ by using subtle skin tones and creams to help you stay hydrated.

10 Of the people I spoke to, none _____ by dieting alone. Most had also followed a strict exercise regime.

VOCABULARY *PLUS*
COMPOUNDS

5 Circle the correct options to compete the text.

Fashions, fads, proverbial flashes in the pan. It seems that every household across the country is, at some point or another, destined to be littered with the discarded remnants of somewhat tacky and ¹_____ cost possessions that once signalled today's biggest trends. ²_____ suffering parents might be inclined to nostalgically muse over the baffling, now broken, ³_____ tech gadgets which once occupied hours of their children's time. Yo-yos, fidget-spinners, loom bands – all ⁴_____ profile pastimes that have now lost their lustre. No doubt to be replaced by a similar and annoyingly ⁵_____ maintenance gimmick which is now all the rage. Over the years, I've been faced with numerous requests for these kinds of toys, and often wondered, sometimes out loud, why they hold such appeal. A ⁶_____ tempered parent

may respond, 'Who cares?', but the psychology of fads is an interesting area of human behaviour. Studies by ⁷_____ powered economists have revealed that when we are faced with a situation where there is limited choice regarding the best product, we tend to look at the behaviour of others and imitate them. Going it alone is considered a ⁸_____ risk strategy, so we feel more comfortable copying the fashions and fads around us. When one influential child in the playground takes up a new fad, then his or her peers will follow suit. And so the herding mentality protects from social embarrassment and reinforces the importance of inclusion. When I asked my ten-year-old daughter for her take on things, she was slightly less ⁹_____ winded. 'Why? Why not? We all like them. It's just … fun.' And so fads, it would seem are here for the ¹⁰_____ haul.

1 a) high **b)** low **c)** long
2 a) long **b)** high **c)** low
3 a) short **b)** long **c)** low
4 a) high **b)** low **c)** short
5 a) high **b)** long **c)** low
6 a) high **b)** low **c)** short
7 a) high **b)** long **c)** low
8 a) short **b)** long **c)** high
9 a) low **b)** long **c)** short
10 a) high **b)** short **c)** long

6 Underline the correct alternative to complete the compounds.

1 This week sees the release of the *long/short* awaited sequel to 1982's sci-fi classic.

2 According to the *long/short* range forecast, tomorrow's weather should be good.

3 Although fans had been expecting great things for the final date of the tour, the concert was a rather *high/low* key affair.

4 She'll be off work for the rest of the week, but it's nothing too serious – just a *high/low* grade fever.

5 We've been incredibly *long/short* staffed this week. Unfortunately, we've not been able to process your order.

6 It's not the kind of place where I'd usually shop. It's quite a *high/low* end boutique, and the extortionate prices match.

7 We're trying to limit the number of *long/short* haul flights we do in a year. We find them thoroughly exhausting.

VOCABULARY

FASHION AND LOOKS

1 Match the sentence halves.

1 Despite the technical challenges and inclement weather, the fashion

2 I really wouldn't wear shoes like that – they went

3 He wasn't the most attractive actor, but his incredibly

4 Try as I might, I can't feel that sorry for fashion

5 I would definitely agree that the industry as a whole is responsible for distorting

6 While she's interested in dressing well, I wouldn't say that she

7 Now that the kids have gone to school, they're becoming more fashion

8 Single-breasted suits are a classic cut; it won't be long until they are back

9 Would you look at that magazine cover! There's no way that image

10 I always thought that he was in his 30s, but looks can be

a) hasn't been retouched. Nobody has skin like that!

b) society's view of what a beautiful woman is.

c) conscious and there are certain brands that they avoid like the plague.

d) out of fashion years ago.

e) photogenic features made him a regular in the fashion pages of the day.

f) in fashion, and showing up on the catwalk.

g) deceiving. It's possible that he's much older than that.

h) particularly follows the latest fashions.

I) shoot took place In February to ensure the photographer had the best light.

j) victims who blow their savings on something that is in style for mere weeks.

READING

2 Read the article. Are the statements below true (T) or false (F) according to the writer?

Me, my selfie and I

Search 🔍

There is one ubiquitous feature of social media that seems to truly stand the test of time, a form that lasts longer than other fads, memes and fleeting crazes. It is, of course, the selfie. A recent study revealed that around 90 percent of women's profile pictures, and 54 percent of men's, make use of a selfie. So, what does our propensity for pout-mouthed portraiture say about how we want to be regarded? And what do these images convey to others?

Research has provided some fascinating perspectives on identity and perception. Evidently, when asked to assess a series of images in terms of how photogenic they are, adherents of selfie culture tend to view pictures that they have taken themselves as more attractive than images of them captured by others. Conversely, when the same group was asked to evaluate a disparate collection of online images, they showed bias against selfies. Test subjects tended to rate people depicted in selfies as less trustworthy or socially attractive than those in standard photography. Research also indicated that while nearly 80 percent of people surveyed regularly took selfies, 82 percent would prefer fewer such images on social media. It would appear that we love to take selfies but hate to see selfies that others take!

Psychologists have postulated that this occurs due to our cultural understanding of what a selfie means. For the individual, the image is a genuine act of self-expression while other people's selfies signify self-advertising or narcissism. This is known as a self-serving bias, a cognitive or perceptual process that is distorted by the need to maintain and enhance self-esteem. As we allow this bias to affect us, we show a tendency to perceive ourselves in an overly favourable manner – and in doing so critique others.

Interestingly though, there are patterns to our online behaviour that show while we may wish to be perceived as an individual, we do follow fashions when it comes to taking selfies and the majority of us choose to be depicted in very similar ways.

On the whole, men tend to photograph themselves from below, giving their jaw greater prominence, a feature conventionally associated with power or masculinity. Women's profile selfies are usually photographed from slightly above the eyeline. This affects the viewer's perception of head to body proportions – making the person depicted seem to weigh less. So, while we might think that we are are curating our own image on our terms, in reality, we tend to play out age-old gender stereotypes.

1 The selfie is a transitory craze which will eventually become outmoded.

2 People have the same perception of selfie images of themselves as of others.

3 Surveys into attitudes about selfies provide a compelling insight into human behaviour.

4 People tend to view their own selfies as a method of self-promotion.

5 We often interpret other people's expressions in selfies negatively.

6 People aspire to portray an image of originality, but selfies are influenced by the latest trends.

7 Men and women have the same considerations when it comes to taking selfies.

8 The selfie isn't a mode of self-expression free from conventions and clichés.

GRAMMAR
FRONTING, HEADERS AND TAILS

3 Rewrite each sentence with a suitable header or tail.

1 Trainers like that are pretty hard to come by.
They _____ .

2 Claire's a really stylish individual.
She _____ .

3 Is that apartment where your cousin lives?
That _____ .

4 My friend Anna loves going round markets and getting bargains.
Going _____ .

5 My brother's really happy at work now.
He _____ .

6 Moving to live abroad has been a long-term goal of mine.
It _____ .

7 What keeps her motivated is going to the gym.
Going _____ .

8 Can you remember where you first heard this song?
This _____ .

4 Complete the conversation with words and phrases in the box. There are two extra items you don't need.

| it   it's a   pretty warm   remember where   that |
| that   there's a   this one   those   what it's |

A: Very stylish, ¹_____ jacket. How much was it?

B: A couple of hundred pounds ²_____ cost me.

A: New?

B: No, ³_____, I've had it for ages.

A: Is it merino wool? ⁴_____ that stuff.

B: ⁵_____ made of, I have no idea.

A: ⁶_____ you bought it, do you?

B: ⁷_____ I do. It was in Manchester.

A: Right! ⁸_____ great place, Manchester, don't you think?

B: Yeah, lovely city.

WRITING
A DESCRIPTION; LEARN TO USE FRONTING

5 A Read the description. When do you think the description occurs? Why?

a) in the past
b) in the present
c) in the future

¹We climbed steadily, our pace now slowed by the heat of the midday sun. ²Xeno scrambled up the slope more urgently, ignoring our warnings of loose rock and steep drops. Each eager footfall marked the dust, leaving staccato tracks as excitement mounted. After a short time, the brush began to thin, ³and we were suddenly in a clearing, light-scorched retina adjusting to our new surroundings. We put down our packs and walked towards the edge. ⁴An outcrop of rock jutted out from the hillside and offered views for mile upon mile.

⁵We looked down from our vantage point and saw the broad valley spread out below us. A scattering of shelters, their flimsy walls of scavenged wood offering a splash of colour. Beyond that, a vast expanse of sand. ⁶A large, skeletal building stood on the edge of the desert. ⁷The burnished roof gleamed in the harsh light and looked like a candle moments before it gutters and dies. Tiny, slender figures, like ghosts or wind-blown smoke, toiled in the shade it offered. ⁸There was a great heap of machinery ahead of them, which they picked through. Harvesting remains, searching for whatever fuel they could find.

⁹A shrill cry came from among the rocks behind us, momentarily causing panic. The crackle and hiss of static, and then the voice over the radio. Our signal.

'Come on, it's time we left, our work is done.'

'Wait. One more second. Tell me, what did they call this place?'

'Earth. They called it Earth.'

B Rewrite the underlined phrases in the description using fronting.

C Which of the sentences you rewrote include an adverb at the beginning of the clause and which include a prepositional phrase?

D Write a description of your own (220–280 words) for a university creative writing magazine. Write about a person or place. Use some of the ideas from this unit to help you.

VOCABULARY
WELL-BEING

1 Complete the texts with the words and phrases in the box.

> cure-all   exert myself physically
> get engrossed in
> incorporate into my daily routine
> magic bullet   out of synch with myself
> panacea   restoring my piece of mind

A

I suppose I didn't really get into it until I was recuperating from an injury. Sport and exercise have always been important to me, but up to that point it was predominantly something I'd ¹_____ – a run during my lunch hour, or maybe a bit of swimming to wind down after work. My physio explained that to build up any lost muscle mass I had to ²_____, so that's when I started looking at high-intensity options. Lifting weights has helped a great deal, but it's no ³_____; you need to consider the way you look after yourself holistically.

B

For me, taking up tai-chi was all about ⁴_____ – I needed something to give me a bit more balance, and help to provide a welcome rest from the anxieties of everyday life. I work in a high-pressure results-driven environment, so stress is constant. Last year came the crunch. I just felt so ⁵_____ that getting out of bed each day was a challenge. Fortunately, a close friend turned me on to it. From this vantage point, I can certainly say that any form of rest and reflection does you the world of good. Meditative activities are a bit of a ⁶_____.

C

Trail running has been a revelation to me. Jogging and park running have their place, but compared with getting out there in the hills and woodland, they are a second best. It's one of those activities that you can ⁷_____ so easily. Working out different routes, checking weather forecasts or deciding on what gear you need for each excursion. But, once you are pounding through the wilderness you feel incredibly alive. Having said that, it's certainly not a ⁸_____ – I've probably picked up more knocks in the last six months than any time running on city streets.

FUNCTION
INFORMAL TURN-TAKING

2 Underline the correct alternative to complete the sentences.

1 As I was *saying/telling* before you interrupted, it's a really good opportunity to find out about the latest fashions.

2 Going *on/back* to your studies, have you thought anymore about what you want to write your thesis on?

3 Like I *told/said*, there's no point doing all that work and then just giving up the first time it gets difficult.

4 I just *want/wish* to add a few points about that, too. Have you thought about the cost?

5 Oh, I *mean/meant* to add that there are lots of opportunities to explore the nightlife, too.

6 Good point. *Apparently/Actually* that's like something I read online this afternoon.

7 Oh that *reminds/remembers* me. I heard that 90s stuff is back in fashion.

8 Funny you should *tell/mention* that. I read an article saying much the same thing.

LEARN TO
JUSTIFY YOUR POSITION

3 A Put the underlined words in the correct order to complete the conversation.

A: So, I hear that you've been following a Paleo diet recently. What's that all about then? Isn't it loading up on protein, and getting all prehistoric? What's the appeal of eating like a caveman?

B: ¹about / just / it's / not eating meat, there's a bit more to it than that. It's more to do with excluding or avoiding anything that is processed – and there's no dairy, added salt or sugar. You only eat things Paleolithic people would have had, about 10,000 years ago …

A: Sounds like it's very limiting. Why would you want to put yourself through something like that?

B: Well, ²from / loss / apart / the / weight, proven / for / benefits / does / it / have increasing energy levels. It's a pretty healthy option, overall.

A: Really? I would have thought that you'd be missing out on all the vitamins and minerals from dairy stuff.

B: Well, you get plenty of those from fresh fruit and nuts. And seafood. That's a big part of the diet. I really do think Paleo ³forward / the / is / way.

A: Well, if you ask me, it sounds like a fad. I'm sure that modern food production can't be all that bad. And aren't there really valuable nutrients in wheat products? You can't be eating any of those.

B: ⁴tried / if / you've / but / it / don't / I / know you can get lots of nutrients from raw seaweed. It's a bit tricky to track down, but I've got a tub of stuff from the local beach.

A: No thanks, I think I'll stick to my usual 21st-century snacks.

B: Don't be so dismissive. ⁵is / advantage / like / something / the / of / this you'll lose weight quickly, and feel more energised.

A: And end up with skin like a cavewoman. Great! ⁶I've / found / is / what / works / me / really / for a nice pasta salad!

B ▶ 5.2 Listen and check.

VOCABULARY

CITIES

1 Match the sentence halves.

1 I've never been bothered by the hustle and bustle of life in Berlin;
2 There are a couple of areas I'd call no-go zones
3 Town planners are concerned that the new urban design is too alienating;
4 I miss the buzz of living in the city centre;
5 Life in New York's been hard. It's so hectic;
6 I really enjoy having all these great places to eat on my doorstep;
7 If you're looking for a little bit of sanctuary,
8 I felt out of place living in that area downtown;

a) the local park is a tranquil place to hang out.
b) everybody's always on the move.
c) to be honest, it's less congested than most European cities.
d) you are spoilt for choice in this neighbourhood.
e) there was so much going on, wherever you were.
f) I think I'm more suited to living in the suburbs.
g) but it's not that intimidating; it's generally a laid-back place.
h) some older residents no longer feel like the city is theirs.

READING

2 A Is the writer optimistic or pessimistic about the future of cities? Read the article and find out.

WHERE ARE WE GOING TO LIVE NEXT?

Growing numbers of us are still moving into cities. The United Nations estimates that by 2050 some 66 percent of the planet's population will live within urban areas. Much of the expected growth will take place in countries of the developing regions, particularly Africa. As a result, these countries will face numerous challenges in meeting the needs of their expanding urban populations.

1 _____

While many people might well consider the idea of living in a city of the future as a <u>daunting</u> prospect, urban planners are looking at ways to rise to the occasion. The combination of climate change and creative solutions offered by new technology could allow for interesting approaches to urban improvement. The future may not be as <u>bleak</u> as anticipated. In fact, material scientists are keen to explore the potential of the city as a playground.

2 _____

As well as addressing energy needs, innovative materials can impact on health. Quieter roads would mean a substantial reduction in urban noise, which is a contributing factor to both stress and heart disease.

But it's not just about dealing with pollution. Climate change issues can be tackled, too.

As urban temperatures increase, this heat could be <u>harnessed</u> to grow a variety of different plant species on rooftops, creating produce which could be used to feed the growing population, and provide greater biodiversity.

3 _____

But what about more immediate changes? According to recent studies, there are two main factors which are currently driving the quest for urban improvement – population density and education. This supports traditional theories of urban change, which suggest that a high concentration of well-educated residents is important when pushing developers to make changes which will benefit the overall populace.

4 _____

Technology also requires funding if future cities are <u>to flourish</u>. We live in a time of connectivity, where billions of devices and household objects are linked, sending data that shapes every element of urban life. There is no better example of this than in the smart cities which are growing around the world.

5 _____

Cities like Songdo in South Korea go even further, with the city itself <u>anticipating</u> the behaviour and preferences of its residents, and changing their experience of it accordingly. But, as with urban planning, it is vital that residents of smart cities have their say. As Francesca Bria, chief innnovations officer based in Barcelona, puts it, the city is not just a digital model. She believes that cities of the future will be at least partially self-governing and their residents will participate directly in budgeting, planning and managing key projects that affect their everyday lives.

* WHO: World Health Organisation

B Read the article again. Five paragraphs have been removed. Match paragraphs A–F with gaps 1–5. There is one extra paragraph which you do not need to use.

A According to urban engineer Joris Voeten, these gardens can also reduce rooftop temperatures by up to 40°C, greatly cooling the overall urban environment. An additional benefit is that plants act as filters, removing pollutants caused by traffic congestion. Long-term, these green screens could return clean air to many choked up cities.

B In these urban environments, the flow of information helps authorities to improve transport infrastructure in real time, reduce costs and make more efficient the day-to-day running of services. In London, Barcelona and New York, bus schedules and services change based on current use. In Singapore and Dubai, driverless cars navigate the streets.

C Working with large companies that use this research data to shape design is an important way of preparing cities for the growth they will see. One drawback is that the information may be commercially sensitive. Balancing the rights of residents with development is a challenge and some urban planning groups are concerned about the implications for individual privacy.

D This scenario is causing concern among global aid agencies and the WHO*. As the urban population swells, there will be an increased pressure on housing, employment, energy and other essential services. Further to this, issues such as climate change are placing additional demands on already stretched urban environments.

E There is an assumption that the better the education system, the more critically residents will think about change. Being able to assess and evaluate plans in terms of their long- and short-term impact makes for more engaged residents. While some urban planners may not embrace this approach of collective planning, it has proved to result in more liveable cities. So, investment in education is a key factor and may be vital for the success of urban development.

F So, what can we expect to find in a city of the future? Carbon-capturing buildings, photovoltaic pavements, and noise-dampening road surfaces are all in their infancy, but these innovations will all be incorporated. Computer models have already shown how much energy could be generated if every rooftop in major urban areas had solar panels in place.

C Match the people or organisations 1–5 with the views a)–e).
1 The WHO
2 Material scientists
3 Joris Voeten
4 Urban planners
5 Francesca Bria

a) Some of the results of climate change can be exploited to lessen its impact.
b) It's not always worthwhile seeking the opinions of city residents.
c) Accelerated urban growth could impact on infrastructure, particularly in developing countries.
d) A combination of modern technology and resident input is the best way forward for future cities.
e) Cities provide considerable opportunity for exploring new design concepts.

3 Match the underlined words in the article with the definitions.
1 with little hope _____
2 to prosper _____
3 a hypothesis, belief _____
4 a description of a situation _____
5 extremely difficult, intimidating _____
6 controlled, exploited _____
7 predicting, foreseeing _____

GRAMMAR
CONCESSION CLAUSES

4 Underline the correct alternative to complete the sentences.
1 Shy *although/as* I am, I want to get out and meet more local people.

2 They told me I was a very competent speaker, but they're just being polite, *though/despite*.

3 Poor as my cooking is, I *do/will* like it when people enjoy what I make.

4 We live in an apartment close to the historic centre, *albeit/though* a very small one.

5 As exciting *as/although* life here is, there are times when you want a bit of quiet.

6 *Albeit/However* interesting it may seem, there are drawbacks to the job.

7 She is always encouraging me, *despite/even though* I think she's not convinced I'll ever be able to drive.

8 Keen traveller *as/although* I am, there are some places I just wouldn't want to visit.

5 Read the article. Find and correct eight mistakes with concession clauses.

¹Self-styled city boy although I am, I couldn't help finding Yoshino Mountain a fascinating place to spend a few days. ²Despite the fact of the hilltop town is only a couple of hours from the ancient capital of Nara, in the off-season it's rarely visited. ³In spring, when the famed sakura are in blossom, hordes of tourists visit to admire the thousands of cherry trees in full bloom. ⁴Even though I was there in late October. ⁵Jam-packed when it can be, Yoshino has still managed to retain the charm and relative tranquillity of many rural retreats. ⁶Albeit, there are a growing number of ryokan (guest houses) competing for the tourist yen. ⁷Important if it is to have the opportunity to rest somewhere with a warm bed and wi-fi, my particular destination was the Kizo-in, a Buddhist temple close to the Zao-do hall. ⁸The second largest wooden structure in Japan, in 2004 this was designated a UNESCO World Heritage Site. ⁹Its scale is breathtaking, and given the mountain-top location it looks awe-inspiring. ¹⁰However indifferent you can be about faith or even architecture, there are times when you just can't deny the impact a building can have upon people. ¹¹In the half-light of the evening, people walked around the grounds in silence, quietly reflecting on their place in the world. ¹²I enjoyed a small, even though tasty, meal with visting monks before heading back to my lodgings. ¹³The next day I would climb the mountain, and set out into the forests beyond.

VOCABULARY *PLUS*

BINOMIALS

6 Circle the correct option to complete the sentences.

1 Sooner _____ later, property prices in cities become unaffordable for locals.
a) and **b)** in **c)** or

2 Some kids sprayed graffiti on the community centre after they were told to leave. It was just tit _____ tat.
a) but **b)** for **c)** or

3 All _____ all, the quality of life in a city like Copenhagen has improved of late.
a) and **b)** for **c)** in

4 This year's make _____ break for the local council; they need to solve the traffic congestion problem.
a) and **b)** or **c)** in

5 Large crowds and traffic jams are just part _____ parcel of modern life, aren't they?
a) but **b)** for **c)** and

6 Slowly _____ surely things have been changing round here. It's becoming a safer area.
a) and **b)** but **c)** or

7 They were worried that the kids were out somewhere in this weather, but they were here all along – safe _____ sound.
a) and **b)** but **c)** in

8 The regeneration programme has been more _____ less a success, but there are still improvements to be made.
a) and **b)** in **c)** or

9 First _____ foremost, you need to think about whether you can afford to pay the rent.
a) or **b)** but **c)** and

10 They've opened some great restaurants near the station. It's a perfect place to wine _____ dine clients.
a) or **b)** and **c)** in

7 Complete the sentences with the correct binomials from Exercise 6.

1 The police are worried about a series of _____ attacks by gangs.

2 I'd _____ your friends at that fantastic new Italian place if you want to impress them.

3 _____, moving to London was the best thing that she ever did.

4 It's _____ time for our company. We need this contract or we'll go bust.

5 _____ they are going to have to knock that old building down. It's an eyesore.

6 Late nights are _____ of being a new parent. But it gets easier with time.

7 We better let her know we're home _____ as she worries if we don't get in touch.

8 _____ the flat is starting to feel like a home. We've done a lot to it since we moved in.

9 _____ I think of myself as a New Yorker. It's a city with a strong identity.

10 They've _____ finished the work on the underground system. It's much better now.

LISTENING

1 A You are going to listen to an interview. Look at the pictures. Predict what the interviewee does for a job.

B ▶ 6.1 Listen and check.

C Listen again and choose the correct option to answer the questions.

1 What are the possible results if the speaker does a good job?
   a) People will find the films amusing and entertaining.
   b) She will be rewarded financially.
   c) The film could become prestigious or win a prize.

2 How has foreign-language cinema changed according to the speaker?
   a) The plotlines have become more complex and confusing.
   b) The language used is less formal and more colloquial.
   c) They tend to feature more elaborate costumes.

3 What does the speaker have to most bear in mind as she works?
   a) How the film-makers want to convey certain ideas.
   b) How the audience will react to her choice of wording.
   c) How any differences in UK and US language could be misinterpreted.

4 According to the speaker, why is it important to have two lines per screen?
   a) You can only use a limited number of words on screen.
   b) Viewers can't read any more than that.
   c) Viewers complain that subtitles may block the action.

5 What does the speaker say is especially difficult about dealing with gestures?
   a) They have a variety of meanings across cultures.
   b) There are too many of them used in modern cinema.
   c) They can be key to illustrating the storyline.

6 Why does the speaker believe her job is satisfying?
   a) It's very well-paid and not over challenging.
   b) She feels priviledged to work in the world of film.
   c) The effect her work has on other people can be rewarding.

D Listen again. Complete the sentences with no more than three words.

1 Get it wrong, and the most _____ becomes a laugh-out-loud comedy.

2 You need to use a lot of creativity with subtitles, otherwise the audience will just _____.

3 Something that might shock an audience in the UK or US could be _____ in other parts of the world.

4 Especially when you _____ as much as possible with the audio track.

5 Across countries and cultures, there are _____ in meaning …

6 And in _____, it's pretty good, so that's a bonus factor, too.

VOCABULARY

SUMMARISING VERBS

2 For 1–7, complete the second sentence so it has a similar meaning to the first. Use no more than five words and the word given.

1 The aid agency is promising to do all it can to help resolve the situation. VOW
   The aid agency _____ help resolve the situation.

2 The government are requesting an inquiry into the shortage of qualified translators. CALL FOR
   A government inquiry _____ into the shortage of qualified translators.

3 Students expressed their worries about the quality of the education they received. VOICE
   Students _____ about the quality of their education.

4 He keeps saying that he hasn't done anything illegal. MAINTAIN
   He _____ nothing wrong.

5 I think that the issue just shows their weakness. ILLUSTRATE
   The issue continues _____ weak they've become.

6 The translator got told off after going off script during the conference. REPRIMAND
   The translator _____ following the script during the conference.

7 The bank admitted to making errors with the account for several years. ACKNOWLEDGE
   The bank _____ been making mistakes for several years.

GRAMMAR

INDIRECT SPEECH

3 Correct the mistakes in the sentences.

1 The speaker at the conference insisted in speaking English, although he had an interpreter.
_____

2 They suggested me to go for extra lessons to improve my speaking.
_____

3 To be honest, I regret to tell her anything about it.
_____

4 She says she don't hear anything. I think she must have been sleeping.
_____

5 I couldn't understand what he did write. It was so difficult.
_____

6 Your father advised to talk to a lawyer about the situation.
_____

7 I told him that if we left late we will miss the train.
_____

8 The board of directors discussed if they should terminate his contract.
_____

9 He recommend them stay somewhere close to the airport.
_____

10 We asked him give us a call when you arrive home.
_____

4 Report the conversations using the verbs in the box.

| advise   complain   deny   explain   insist   warn |

1

Anna: Come on; get ready now! You've got to go! Your meeting starts at two.

Peter: OK, OK, don't rush me! Look, I'm just choosing what to wear.

Anna: And you'd better take a taxi – it'll be quicker. Don't be late again or you'll be in real trouble.

Peter: I've never been late for an appointment. Ever.

_____

_____

_____

| assure   promise   remind   warn |

2

Chiara: So, you remember that you're coming to ours for dinner tomorrow?

Paul: Sure, I'll definitely be there for eight.

Chiara: Oh, and by the way, Dad's making a really spicy stew – just so you are prepared!

Paul: Don't worry about me. I can eat just about anything.

_____

_____

_____

WRITING

SYNTHESISING FROM DIFFERENT SOURCES

5 A Read the question and make notes on your opinion.

Which is more valid and reliable in the modern age: a human translator or a digital translation tool?

B Read two short extracts about translating. Identify the source.

Extract 1 _____

Ast Translation Services

You will be part of our In-house translation team, working closely with an overseas language office team. You will be responsible for delivering translations of the highest quality and accuracy on time and within budget. You will have the opportunity to act as Lead Translator for one or several accounts and to support the development of your translation team members.

Our current client list includes the World Health Organization (WHO) and the World Bank. Your translations will be used to provide information and documents for medical staff and support staff in many of the world's most challenging developing regions.

Extract 2 _____

⊙ sign in   ⊙ search

One of the biggest challenges facing translators today is explaining our relevance in a world where digital tools are becoming more and more capable of doing our job. Often people are asked, 'Why don't your clients just use Google Translate?' Given that artificial intelligence (AI) is developing quickly, and online resources are improving, this is a valid question. So, what are the answers? Well, a typical translator's response might be that issues with word order, verb choice and tone will always mean digital tools are second best. But perhaps more importantly, online translations are extremely literal – they lack context. Think of any idiomatic phrase in a language you know well. Understanding often requires knowledge of history, culture and social interaction. And that is something an app may never achieve.

C Write an essay that answers the question in Exercise 5A (250 words). Use ideas from the extracts in Exercise 5B and your own ideas from Exercise 5A. Use a range of linking words to make your writing cohesive.

VOCABULARY
CONVENTIONS

1 Complete the text with the words and phrases in the box.

> atypical   commonplace   customary   expected
> inappropriate   out of the ordinary   peculiar to
> routine   taken for granted   unheard of

The first couple of months that I spent in Russia saw me make a series of faux pas. I suppose, to an extent, when your'e travelling in European capitals it's ¹_____ that there are a number of shared customs and conventions, but you forget just how different things are elsewhere. Really, nothing should be ²_____. I was an undergrad in St Petersburg when I first met Alexei. We got on well, and enjoyed discussing philosophy and literature. As is ³_____ in these situations, he eventually invited me to his house to have dinner with his parents. This is a fairly ⁴_____ occurrence for exchange students, so I thought I'd pull it off without causing any diplomatic incidents. Unfortunately, I was young and didn't realise then what you have to do when you go to dinner in Russia – you see, there are quite clear rules. It's all very ⁵_____, but in my enthusiasm I didn't bother to find out about them. First, I took some flowers – nothing ⁶_____ there, surely? Sadly, my choice of blooms was totally ⁷_____. For Russians, yellow flowers symbolise the end of a relationship. Alexei didn't look overly happy when I gave his mother a bunch of yellow roses. The next thing I did wrong was to keep my outdoor shoes on. I suppose that's not ⁸_____ in the UK, but I was more concerned about the potential embarrassment of exposing my threadbare socks. I thought it was just a normal family dinner, so I also wore my usual student attire. An exasperated Alexei told me that you really ought to dress well when someone invites you to dinner, as this indicates you think the invitation is important.

When dinner arrived, the food was fantastic. I ate everything on my plate, but was very full. When Alexei's mother offered me more I said 'no thank you'. She looked a bit put out. Evidently that was an ⁹_____ response by guests in the Anishin household. Later, Alexei explained that you need to leave a little food on your plate to show you are finished. I kicked myself for making such an error of judgement. The tradition isn't ¹⁰_____ Russia after all – there are a number of cultures which do the same. Equally, if you refuse more, your host might think you didn't enjoy your meal. Luckily they forgave my lack of manners, and invited me back again …

FUNCTION
TALK ABOUT CUSTOMS

2 A ▶ 6.2 Listen to three people discussing experiences of other cultures. Match each person 1–3 with a topic a)–c).

a) Shopping   **b)** Friendliness   **c)** Eating a meal

B Listen again and complete the extracts.
1 You'd think I'd _____ it by now, I mean, I've been living here since the late 90s.
2 But I just _____ piling all my food on to one plate.
3 When it first happened, I found it a _____ experience.
4 I didn't know at the time, but it's _____ when a new customer comes in they should be welcomed …
5 I come from London, so I _____ people being a bit stand-offish.
6 The _____ help each other out if you possibly can.

3 Use the phrases from Exercise 2B to make sentences about your experiences of other cultures.

LEARN TO
QUESTION GENERALISATIONS

4 A Complete the responses using the prompts in brackets.
1 **A:** I read an online article that says British tourists aren't welcome in the city anymore.
  B: _____, you know, what's the evidence? (always / wonder / thing)
2 **A:** There's a huge problem with online bullying in high schools.
  B: _____. I've never heard of it happening. (still / wonder / common)
3 **A:** Asian people tend to be the most reluctant to speak at meetings, don't they?
  B: _____. I know a lot of very talkative Japanese people. (hear / but / sound / stereotype)
4 **A:** Women are generally much better at listening to others than men.
  B: _____? It's a pretty sweeping statement. (do / think / case)
5 **A:** They'll be really offended if you don't eat what they offer you.
  B: _____. People tend to be aware that not everyone has the same taste. (somehow / doubt / true)

B ▶ 6.3 Listen and check.

GRAMMAR NOUN PHRASES

1 Use the notes and the information in the sentences to rewrite them with noun phrases and as few words as possible.

1 Michael Mosley's diet helped begin a diet revolution around the globe. It promoted the benefit of fasting. (British doctor) (diet was ground-breaking) (5:2 diet) (introduced in 2013) (significant) (health)

_____
_____

2 In 2012, Mosley began high-intensity training. (55-year-old) (out of shape) (made decision) (lost weight) (improved overall fitness)

_____
_____

3 Mosely's revelation that he suffered from insomnia surprised many people. But tests conducted after changing his diet to promote a healthy microbiome showed his sleep quality had improved. (now healthy) (many years) (University of Oxford's Department of Psychiatry) (almost threefold)

_____
_____

VOCABULARY REVIEW 1

2 Complete the text with the phrases in the box.

achieve success   cure-all
deliver a host of benefits   deliver tangible results
incorporate into a daily routine
looks can be deceiving   out of synch with yourself
trigger rapid weight gain

We all know that taking care of what you eat can [1] _____ in terms of health and well-being, but the latest scientific research has shown that even some ostensibly 'healthy' options should be avoided. Our tendency to promote increased fruit and vegetable intake as a [2] _____ could actually be causing more harm than good. Although the ever-increasing range of smoothies and fruit juices available in supermarkets and coffee shops seem a healthier option than that calorific hot chocolate, [3] _____. Many of these have massive amounts of added sugars which can [4] _____ as they stimulate the production of insulin which then stores any available energy as fats. Drink too many of them, and you'll soon feel [5] _____. However, there's no need to despair, there are a few tricks that you can [6] _____ which will promote a healthier lifestyle. One way to [7] _____ is to work on building healthy gut microbiome, which can help reduce weight and give you more energy. Eating food rich in probiotics, like live yoghurt, kimchi and miso soup will [8] _____ by providing the 'good' bacteria that help regulate your body.

GRAMMAR FRONTING, HEADERS AND TAILS

3 Rewrite the sentences starting with the word given.

1 Have they finished that new housing development over by the canal yet?
That _____?

2 He cheats during exams and everyone knows it.
Cheating _____.

3 This group of students are mainly from Singapore.
They _____.

4 Is that black mountain bike leaning against the window yours?
That _____?

5 Our kids aren't really so bad.
They _____.

6 Amanda isn't worth bothering about.
She _____.

7 The fact that so many people have complained is particularly significant.
Particularly _____.

8 The dog, no bigger than a rat, had been left to fend for itself.
Left _____.

VOCABULARY PLUS COMPOUNDS

4 Complete the sentences with the phrases in the box.

high-maintenance   high-powered   high-risk
high-tech   long-haul   long-winded   low-cost
low-profile   short-tempered

1 They made quite a niche for themselves providing _____ solutions for public housing, helping the council save on their budget.

2 It's too much of a _____ strategy. You can't gamble with health and safety like that.

3 Although a best-selling children's author, he's renowned as a _____ and often extremely offensive individual.

4 Those kids are so _____ – they're constantly demanding new stuff. It drives me mad!

5 I have no intention of quitting, I'm in it for the _____.

6 She's quite a _____ figure in the fashion industry – she can make or break a new designer.

7 With its increased opportunities for digital start-ups, this city is set to be one of the most _____ areas in the country.

8 While I really enjoy the snappy dialogue in her novels, the descriptions are so drawn out and _____.

9 Their relatively _____ approach to marketing means that they can spend more on research and development.

FUNCTION INFORMAL TURN-TAKING

5 A Put the underlined words in the correct order to complete the sentences.
   a) him / of / talking, did you hear what happened last week?
   b) mention / should / you / that / funny, I just heard about it on the radio.
   c) was / I / where / anyway? Oh, yes, we need to call the plumber.
   d) back / I / before / saying / was / getting / to / what, can you make it to the party?
   e) saying / what / was / I / anyway?
   f) reminds / me / oh / that. We're meeting them later.
   g) feel / I / way / same / the / about things, to be honest.

B Complete the conversations with the sentences from Exercise 5A.
   1 A: _____
      B: You were talking about the new fashion store in town.
   2 A: I'm considering this 5:2 diet. It sounds like a good option.
      B: _____
   3 A: I'm not happy at all. There have been too many changes.
      B: _____
   4 A: I saw Natasha and Clare at the gym this morning.
      B: _____
   5 A: The new doctor is seeing patients in clinic three.
      B: _____
   6 A: Hmm, yeah, that's interesting, I was thinking about them earlier.
      B: _____
   7 A: Sorry to interrupt, but have you seen the state of the bathroom?
      B _____

VOCABULARY REVIEW 2

6 Complete the pairs of sentences with the correct word or phrase.
   1 hustle and bustle / bit of sanctuary
      a) First time visitors shouldn't miss the _____ of Times Square – a carnival of commerce in the heart of the city.
      b) I've found that there's a small park among the skyscrapers that offers a _____.
   2 alienating / intimidating
      a) The proposed plans envisioned a high-tech city which traditionalists sadly found too _____ to approve.
      b) There are some suburbs where the towering blocks and dark underpasses create an _____ atmosphere.

   3 downtown / a no-go zone
      a) Due to spiralling crime rates, Ramona Beach was declared a _____.
      b) Following a large amount of investment, _____ has become a more attractive area.
   4 pleaded / vowed
      a) He _____ to me that he'd never do anything like that again.
      b) She _____ with her parents to let her go to the party, but they refused.
   5 maintains / acknowledges
      a) The manager _____ that he may have been at fault for the embarrassing defeat.
      b) He _____ his innocence, but it's starting to wear a bit thin.
   6 echoed / voiced
      a) The nursing staff _____ concerns that they were being unfairly treated.
      b) She _____ the opinions of several leading experts.
   7 illustrates / relates
      a) This just _____ the problem. We'll solve nothing without talking.
      b) The article _____ the difficulties faced by many immigrants in Europe.
   8 customary / commonplace
      a) I think that it's sadly going to be an increasingly _____ event.
      b) It's _____ in this part of the world to invite new neighbours for a meal.
   9 atypical / inappropriate
      a) His comments were completely _____; he managed to upset almost everyone.
      b) I think that was fairly _____ behaviour. She's usually well-mannered.
   10 peculiar to / routine in
      a) It's a custom which is _____ the area. They don't do it elsewhere.
      b) That kind of thing is quite _____ these parts. Don't worry about it.

GRAMMAR CONCESSION CLAUSES

7 Complete the text with the words in the box.

> albeit   although   as (x2)   despite   do
> even though   nevertheless   though

Adventurous [1]_____ I am, there are areas of the city I just haven't got to visit yet. [2]_____ living in London for nearly a decade, this is my first time at Trinity Buoy Wharf, an industrial area next to the Thames. [3]_____ it's a dank and fairly unwelcoming evening in late October, the place is absolutely buzzing. Why? Well, it's home to one of the UK's most prominent functional fitness gyms, where you can develop the skills required for anything from free-running to cage-fighting. Now, poor [4]_____ my current fitness levels are, I [5]_____ fancy the idea of being able to confidently run up a wall, [6]_____ a small one, given my height. Or at the very least be better equipped to navigate my surroundings. [7]_____, I'm not naïve enough to try to tackle this on my own, so I've enlisted the assistance of Karl Smith, an expert in urban sports training. [8]_____ Karl is quietly spoken, he pushes me to the absolute limit with a series of circuits and intensive weightlifting exercises. This is before we've even done any balance work [9]_____, so I'm thoroughly shattered by the end of the session!

VOCABULARY PLUS BINOMIALS

8 Underline the correct alternatives.

A Am I happy with the redevelopment project? More [1]*than/or* less, but I would have preferred it if there'd been a little more consultation with local residents. First [2]*and/or* foremost our opinion matters because we have to live here on a daily basis. It's fine to create green spaces on a big estate, but I want to know how they are going to be managed. We don't want them being overrun, and becoming no-go zones. The kids here are mainly a good bunch, but if there is trouble, you know some tit [3]*for/with* tat thing, then it can get messy.

B It always happens, doesn't it? Sooner [4]*than/or* later a local business goes down the tubes and in come the urban trendies. Slowly [5]*yet/but* surely the character of the place changes. Gentrification, isn't it? I know it's part [6]*for/and* parcel of living in a city, but I miss the old ways, you know? That place over there, that was a greengrocer's. Five generations ran it. Now it's a gastro bar. Who's going to wine [7]*and/or* dine anyone around here? Madness!

C I think that this year is make [8]*or/and* break for our firm. We're really hoping to win the contract to renovate the old steelyard quarter. It's got some incredible potential and great charm. We're thinking design vernacular. All [9]*on/in* all this is a super exciting time for us! Anyway, I'd better go. Presentations start at four. I've got the plans safe [10]*and/or* sound here. Somewhere …

GRAMMAR INDIRECT SPEECH

9 Complete the second sentence to report the first using the correct form of the reporting verbs in the box.

> advise   assure   deny   insist   invite
> promise   remind   warn

1 'Don't forget to bring your driving licence, Johan.' Katia said.
Katia _____.

2 'I wouldn't stay in that part of town, it's expensive.' Alex told Clare.
Alex _____.

3 'Why don't you come out for something to eat?' Fotios asked me.
Fotios _____.

4 'Don't go into that area, it's a no-go zone,' the taxi driver told us.
The taxi driver _____.

5 'It's not true that I'm a poor translator,' Mila said.
Mila _____.

6 'Don't worry, you'll have a great time,' the tour guide told me.
The tour guide _____.

7 'I'll pay for the meal, please, it's my treat,' said Hannah.
Hannah _____.

8 'I'll make sure that the essay is in on time,' Orhan told his tutor.
Orhan _____.

FUNCTION TALK ABOUT CUSTOMS

10 Find and correct the mistakes in the sentences. Two sentences are correct.

1 I was unaware of the custom, but evidently it's given that anyone clearing their plate should be offered more food.

2 I found it a completely alien experience; I was so used to people being treated as equals.

3 You think he should be accustomed to it by now. He's lived here since he was a teenager.

4 I'm sorry, but I just can't get used to all the traffic round here. It's crazy.

5 Coming from a city like New York I'm use to people being loud and obnoxious.

6 Over here the normal is to help out with the community whenever possible.

7 Where I come from, it expects that you take a gift when you are invited for a meal.

8 I know it seems a bit strange, but in this part of the world it's custom to share the cost.

CHECK

Circle the correct option to complete the sentences.

1 It's a _____ management team, nothing will go wrong.
   a) highly organised and efficient
   b) high organised and efficient
   c) highly and organised efficient

2 Do you have any _____ for when you leave?
   a) long plans or aspirations
   b) long-terms or aspirations
   c) long-term plans or aspirations

3 In tonight's programme we _____ an aspect of culture which is still underground.
   a) deliver   b) discuss   c) enhance

4 They've found it difficult to _____ interest in the IT course.
   a) deliver   b) achieve   c) sustain

5 As soon as I saw the photos, it _____ a memory of the old house.
   a) delivered   b) triggered   c) enhanced

6 I feel sorry for his _____ -suffering wife. He's such a bore.
   a) low   b) high   c) long

7 You can't just focus on _____ -term gains. What about next year?
   a) high   b) long   c) short

8 We feel a bit _____ changed. Ninety minutes isn't long enough for a film nowadays.
   a) high   b) short   c) long

9 Don't be such a fashion _____ – those shoes are ridiculous!
   a) victim   b) conscious   c) model

10 Are those kind of jeans _____ fashion? They look a bit dated to me.
   a) back in   b) out of   c) of

11 _____ a nice girl, young Tracey.
   a) She   b) Her's   c) She's

12 *La Mundi*? Oh yes, great restaurant is _____.
   a) it   b) that   c) there

13 He reckons that yoga is a _____ to all that stress in life.
   a) panacea   b) cure-all   c) magic bullet

14 I don't want to _____ myself too much. I'll just jog this bit.
   a) exert   b) engross   c) restore

15 As I was _____ your dad yesterday, things have to change.
   a) saying   b) telling   c) remembering

16 There's a great new coffee shop right on my _____.
   a) downtown   b) neighbourhood   c) doorstep

17 Don't you miss the _____ of living in Berlin?
   a) buzz   b) hectic   c) hustle

18 _____ you look at it, it's an expensive place to live.
   a) Albeit   b) However   c) Even though

19 It's a lovely area _____ a bit too quiet at times.
   a) albeit   b) although   c) despite

20 I'd more _____ less given up on her.
   a) on   b) or   c) and

21 Well, all _____ all, it's been an unqualified success.
   a) of   b) on   c) in

22 He's _____ their claims – he says it's a conspiracy against him.
   a) alleging   b) relating   c) repudiating

23 They're bound to _____ some kind of inquiry.
   a) plead for   b) call for   c) vow for

24 My personal trainer _____ me not to overdo the exercise plan.
   a) advised   b) denied   c) insisted

25 I _____ her to phone you, I promise.
   a) reminded   b) recommended   c) suggested

26 Well, that certainly wasn't _____. I'm quite shocked!
   a) atypical   b) expected   c) the ordinary

27 Sometimes people take it for _____ that you know the conventions.
   a) expected   b) customary   c) granted

28 It is unusual, but not totally _____ to behave like that.
   a) commonplace   b) unheard of   c) routine

29 I just find it hard to get accustomed _____ the weather here.
   a) for   b) at   c) to

30 Like I said, the _____ is to leave a tip of up to 15 percent.
   a) normal   b) norm   c) normally

RESULT   /30

7 CLASSICS

VOCABULARY

FILM

1 Complete the sentences with the words in the box.

> an A-lister   chick flick
> female protagonist
> flashback   formulaic plotlines
> heist movie   indie film   plot twist
> road movie   spaghetti western
> supporting cast   universal appeal

1 I watched an amazing _____ last night. It seemed like a straight forward bank robbery, but there was a _____ which turned everything on its head.

2 That _____ was her first project. It had very limited distribution, but she chose it because the _____ was such a strong character.

3 *Django Unchained*, with its depiction of gunslingers, was Tarantino's updated version of the _____. It subverted the genre by using techniques like _____ to establish the characters and their context.

4 If a studio wants a big financial return, it tends to cast _____ in one of the main roles. However, this is no guarantee of a box office hit, so having a strong _____ can help bring critical acclaim.

5 Disney films seem to be successful due to their _____, but they occasionally suffer from _____.

6 A film like *Thelma and Louise* is hard to define – is it a _____ predominantly about two women's growing friendship, or a _____ that explores notions of changing identity in America?

LISTENING

2 A Look at the photos. Who do you think has the most influence over the content of a film?

B ▶ 7.1 Listen to two film journalists talking about test screenings. For questions 1–6, choose the best answer a), b), c) or d) according to what you hear.

1 What is said about the creative process of film-making?
   a) It's very much dependent upon financial returns.
   b) It's dependent upon the creative vision of the director.
   c) It's dependent upon collaboration between a number of stakeholders.
   d) It's dependent fundamentally on test audiences.

2 In terms of traditional test screenings, Emma implies that
   a) the audience responses were often spurious.
   b) the data collected was more trustworthy in the past.
   c) the data collected was less trustworthy in the past.
   d) audiences didn't realise their importance in the process.

3 What view is stated about emergent technology being used in test screenings?
   a) It ensures greater accuracy, and provides greater security for investors in the industry.
   b) It ensures greater accuracy, but can be undermined by technical issues.
   c) It impedes accuracy as it underplays emotional responses.
   d) It overstates the importance of emotional responses.

4 Which factors do the speakers feel are worth considering within test audiences?
   a) their attitude towards technology
   b) their attitude towards change in the film industry
   c) their emotional receptiveness
   d) their background, identity and race

5 What do scans of the brain tell us about audience members when the activity is concurrent?
   a) They are all concentrating on identical subject matter in the film.
   b) They all feel more positive about the film.
   c) They always react to the content in exactly the same way.
   d) They are all more critical about the film.

6 Tony expresses concern that the screen testing process could result in
   a) films that lack any artistic merit.
   b) films that favour spectacle over substance.
   c) films that are overly complex and emotional.
   d) films that are less cognitively engaging.

GRAMMAR

SUBJUNCTIVE

3 Find eight verbs to change to the subjunctive to make the text more formal in style. If the change to the subjunctive does not change the verb form, you can use *should*.

Scriptwriters represented by our union are being forced to make last-minute rewrites without additional payments. In addition, writing credits are being removed from many motion picture credits without permission. It is important that these issues are taken into account by the committee at its earliest convenience. The writer's guild has rejected calls that it amends current guidelines, and requested that the union uses its position to petition for improved terms. If any attempt to breach these terms takes place, we advise that the member refuses to comply and notifies their union representative forthwith. We ask that detailed notes of any exchange are kept for legal purposes. It is imperative that these guidelines are followed by all members.

4 For 1–6, complete the second sentence so it has a similar meaning to the first. Use no more than five words and the word given.

1 Can you go now, please? RATHER
   I _____, thanks.
2 We recommend contacting the press immediately. IS
   Our _____ the press immediately.
3 I'd rather you didn't stay for long at the party. BETTER
   It _____ stay for long at the party.
4 I've had enough of her constant complaining! WISH
   I _____ complaining all the time.
5 The children need to go to bed. TIME
   It's _____ in bed.
6 That's an odd thing for you to say. SHOULD
   It's _____ something like that.

WRITING

A REVIEW; LEARN TO EDIT A COMPLEX TEXT

5 A Read a student's review of the film *Blade Runner 2049*. Match the underlined sections with the tutor's comments below.

Strengths

a) Good use of style in terms of evaluation
b) Succinct – a very brief summary of a convoluted plot
c) Concise reference to the original gives contextualisation of the film in genre
d) Good use of descriptive style, rich language!

Weaknesses

e) Overly wordy, could edit this to have more impact
f) Nice use of rhetorical questions, but limit where possible
g) Could use more cohesive devices to connect ideas and improve style
h) How could you improve descriptive style here?

Blade Runner 2049

[1]1982's *Blade Runner* flopped at the cinema – widely dismissed as a stylish but ultimately empty exercise. A victim of negative test screenings, a rather clunky happy ending was tagged on which was only rectified with the Director's Cut a decade later. That version cemented the film as a masterpiece of modern cinema, to sit alongside classics such as Kubrik's *2001*.

So, a quarter of a century later, what should we expect from a sequel to something so revered? Well, the initial promise is good. Dennis Villeneuve is at the helm, bringing with him [2]a bold vision of a future that is bleak yet familiar. Co-written by the original's screenwriter, Hampton Fancher, the story is taut and cerebral but not without an emotional heft.

The action plays out thirty years after the disappearance of replicant hunter Rick Deckard, who went from destroying androids for the law to falling in love with one. In the interim there's been a 'blackout' – ten days of digital darkness which have wiped replicant production records, and created a blank space in humanity's databases. [3]Into this dystopia comes K, played by a lugubrious Ryan Gosling. K tracks down wayward androids – 'retiring' them for any perceived indiscretions. It's during one of his investigations that he comes across information which will lead him to seek out Deckard, and unearth secrets about what humanity has become.

[4]*Blade Runner 2049* asks big questions. There are no formula style plotlines. The action-fuelled set pieces typical of the genre really work. [5]Throughout the film we are asked, what is it to be a human in the digital era? Does identity amount to anything more than one algorithm jostling with countless others? [6]Roger Deakin shows us how identity and image come together through his great way of filming. Characters gaze at each other through glass screens and see the ghosts of themselves gazing back. [7]Bodies blend and diffuse in dust-blown deserts and teeming neon-lit labyrinths. As K's search mirrors Deckard's early quest, this mirroring becomes more apparent. Perhaps Villeneuve is suggesting that in our culturally-aware climes we are all replicants? [8]Whatever the intention, there is no denying that Villeneuve's vision is a spellbinding blockbuster in scope but much more insightful in it's execution, resulting in it being a worthy addition to the sci-fi pantheon.

B Rewrite and improve the sections that the tutor has highlighted as weaknesses.

C Write a review of a film you have seen. Write a first draft of about 380 words. Then reread your work and decide where edits can be made. Your final version should be about 320 words.

VOCABULARY

RELATIONSHIPS

1 Complete the sentences with the words and phrases in the box.

clicked straightaway	didn't take
meet people halfway	never compromise
put a strain on	rocky	stable

1 When John first joined here I _____ to him at all. He seemed very arrogant, actually.

2 Being in the same office as my wife can occasionally _____ our relationship, but things run pretty smoothly if we stick to 'no work chat' at home.

3 Me and Jonno? Ah, we _____ – shared the same interests in sport, music, all kinds of stuff.

4 Me and my flatmate got on great, but things got a bit _____ between us when his girlfriend kept complaining about the state of our flat.

5 I've been married twice, but my new relationship seems quite _____ – not too many arguments.

6 I've learnt, through bitter experience, that when you're in a relationship, you need to _____. Being able to make concessions is so important, or you're constantly bickering.

7 Some people _____, but giving in isn't a weakness – it shows you can understand someone else's perspective.

READING

2 A Read the article and choose the best option.

a) The writer has no experience with creative writing.

b) The writer has some experience with creative writing but not poetry.

c) The writer has a good deal of experience as a stage performer.

B Read the article again. Are the sentences true (T) or false (F)?

1 Poetry had little relevance to the writer as a teenager.

2 A key feature of slam poetry is its foundation in academic study.

3 In poetry slam competitions there are clear parameters given for poets and judges.

4 According to Cristin Hollander, a good slam poet needs to captivate their public and get a response from them.

5 Many novice slam poets are very quickly able to adopt an authentic performing voice.

6 The writer discovers that repeated rehearsal is a valuable exercise.

●●● ◁▷

Neither rhyme nor reason   💬 23

I can hear my pulse pounding, and, through the microphone clenched in my shaking fist, the sound of a strained breath. I look out at the expectant audience, the table of stern judges, ceiling fans in slow rotation. Everyone waits. Waits for words. My head is a torrent of them, but my mouth will not engage. What on earth rhymes with *High Wycombe* …?

Three weeks ago, the term 'poetry slam' meant very little to me. Poetry was one of those rarefied art forms that other people do. Yes, I'd dallied with blank verse as a lovelorn teen, but those were more inspired by favoured songwriters of the time. And fairly ineffective as I recall. Reading poetry was something we were cajoled into by teachers, who then regretted it as our monotones mangled their cherished texts. Why would anyone want to perform it aloud?

Yet they do. In their droves. Beginning from fairly humble roots in Chicago in the mid-80s, where its more competitive, often confrontational nature was intended to move poetry recitals from academia to a popular audience, poetry slams are now a global phenomenon. Bolstered by the conflation of hip-hop flows into more conventional poetic tropes, its mainstream appeal is wider than ever.

The format of poetry slams is a fairly fixed one. Three to five members of the audience are chosen by an MC to act as judges. After each poem is recited, each judge awards a score ranging from zero to ten. The highest and lowest scores are dropped, leaving each performance with their rating. As poets move through the rounds, the lowest scorer is eliminated. There are strict rules regarding props, costumes and musical accompaniment – all forbidden. And you can't overrun the three-minute time limit. Brevity is the key.

To guide me through my first slam, I enlisted the assistance of Cristin Hollander, award-winning slam poet. So, what is the secret to being a success? Cristin's answer seemed to be deceptively simple – 'engage the audience, elicit a reaction'. Hollander reckons that the best way to do this is to imbue your words with your own experiences, foreground your cultural background, and articulate the interplay of this with the world around. Sounds easy enough!

Several hours later, I have a crumpled page before me – scrawlings and strikethroughs, all interpolated with odd doodles and notes on pace. I read my first attempt. Cristin generously nods. Her verdict? 'I've heard worse.' So, it's back to working in rhyme schemes and excising clunky phrases. 'OK, now read it, with a bit of emotion.' Casting off inhibitions I begin. Cristin starts laughing. My error? 'Slam voice' – a rather derisive label for the over-emoting that can go on at spoken word events. One way to discern a newbie is to listen out for high pitch, strained intonation. There's a propensity to push the emotion a bit much, leading to overemphasising words when they are bereft of much meaning. Cristin says it commonly occurs when people watch slam poets in performance and attempt to immediately emulate their style.

A few hours of embarrassment pass, and as I recite my words for the umpteenth time Cristin solemnly intones, 'Yeah, that's it.' And that is how I end up here, on the stage, in the backroom of a pub in East London. I take the mic in my clammy hand, and look out at the audience. A moment, a sigh, then come the words …

GRAMMAR
ADVERBIALS

3 Correct the mistakes in the sentences.

1 I found it quite astonish that so few of my classmates had read his poetry.

_____

2 Starting out as an actress, she has operated as a high success director for the last decade.

_____

3 If you haven't seen the film already, I would thorough recommendation.

_____

4 I was somehow sad to hear that you won't be joining us for dinner this evening.

_____

5 Although the critics don't seem to agree, I thought she was absolute perfect for the part.

_____

6 I think that this piece of music is deep evocation from a time of great sadness.

_____

7 Difficulty as it is to believing, Sarah was given the job despite being the weakest candidate.

_____

8 She only vague remembered me, which I found deep upset.

_____

4 Decide which sentence, a) or b), has a similar meaning to the first.

1 The festival concluded with a fireworks display, which was quite spectacular.
   a) At the end of the festival there was a fairly entertaining fireworks display.
   b) At the end of the festival there was an extremely entertaining fireworks display.

2 On the whole, I'd consider myself as quite a positive individual.
   a) I think of myself as being fairly positive.
   b) I think of myself as extremely positive.

3 The facilities at the hotel were totally inadequate.
   a) I'm rather disappointed that the facilities were below standard.
   b) I'm extremely angry that the facilities were below standard.

4 Despite there being a school nearby, it's a relatively quiet neighbourhood.
   a) Although we live close to the school, it's always quiet round here.
   b) Although we live close to the school, it's mostly quiet round here.

5 Much to my amusement, the team failed to score any goals.
   a) I found it funny that the team lost.
   b) People laughed at me because the team lost.

6 Difficult as it is to believe, she wrote her first novel at the age of sixteen.
   a) People are surprised that she could write a novel at her age.
   b) People don't believe that she could write a novel at her age.

7 On reflection, that was the entirely wrong thing to say.
   a) Thinking about it, I shouldn't have said that.
   b) Thinking about it, those were the wrong words to use.

8 So many of these songs are just instantly forgettable.
   a) I find it hard to remember the words to the songs.
   b) I think that the songs have no lasting value.

VOCABULARY *PLUS*
ADVERB-ADJECTIVE COLLOCATIONS

5 Match words from boxes A and B to make the most appropriate collocation to complete the sentences.

A

bitterly fundamentally greatly hopelessly infinitely predominantly prohibitively vitally

B

admired different disappointed expensive female important inadequate preferable

1 While many people downplay the relevance of poetry in the modern world, I think it's _____ that we have a connection with literature.

2 We'd hoped to get tickets for the premiere of his latest film, but it sold out within seconds. We're _____ that we'll miss it.

3 I've often thought about eating there, but from what I've heard it's _____. The level of service may not match the price tag.

4 The poets on this term's reading list are _____, which will make things interesting when assessing the role of gender and language.

5 There's absolutely no point in trying to compare big studio blockbusters with authentic indie films, they're just _____.

6 I thoroughly enjoyed the trek, but Mark complained the whole time. His boots were _____ for the job, and he ended up with blisters.

7 I'm not really keen on going anywhere in this weather, but heading out is _____ to staying here.

8 Although she's never won a major award, she's _____ by both critics and her peers.

VOCABULARY

TRAVEL

1 Complete the text with the words in the box.

| authentic   indigenous   legendary |
| opulent   panoramic   soaring |
| tranquil   turbulent |

The Tongariro Alpine Crossing

They call it New Zealand's greatest day walk, and having completed the almost 20-kilometre journey, I can see why. Despite the relatively short length, the trek takes you up some pretty rugged terrain, with steep slopes and uneven surfaces adding to the challenge. Not far beneath you [1]_____ forces of nature are shaping and shaking the landscape. Tongariro is a complex of multiple volcanic cones constructed over a period of 275,000 years. While the last eruption of note was in late 2012, wandering below [2]_____ volcanic peaks can make you more than a little apprehensive. But the risk, albeit negligible, is well worth it. Once along the highest ridges there are [3]_____ views stretching out into the distance – on a clear day you can even see as far as Mount Taranaki. Yet it's not just about the heights. As you descend into the Central Crater you find the [4]_____ Emerald and Blue Lakes. These offer a perfect place to stop and reflect on the power of nature. One word of caution, though. The Blue Lake is, according to the [5]_____ Maori people, a sacred site – so eating and drinking around its shore is forbidden.

The crossing has an almost [6]_____ status among the trekking community. But in this case, it's definitely worthy of the praise. Time your trip right and you will certainly have an [7]_____ alpine walking experience. And once you finish? Well, it depends on your budget, but we opted for one night in a rather [8]_____ hotel in nearby Taupo with a very big bath to soak aching limbs.

FUNCTION

TELLING ANECDOTES

2 Complete the story with the words and phrases in the box.

| Funny   I think it was   It was one of those things   some |
| sort of   Strange   stuff like that   this   was like (x2) |
| were like (x2)   you know what I mean? |

[1]_____ you should mention it, but that reminds me of the time when a bunch of us were in Kurashiki. We'd just finished cycling across the Kibi Plains, looking at the different ancient temples and pagodas – you know all the cultural [2]_____. Well, Marta was with us, and she [3]_____ 'When are we going to get something to eat?' Marta's always hungry, [4]_____ So, we wandered about these side streets looking for a place to get something. I was up for getting sushi, but the others [5]_____ 'Can we have something a bit more normal?' I think maybe we'd overdone the traditional food thing. Anyway, after a while, we see [6]_____ place that does curry rice, things like that – a bit shabby looking, but decent enough. So, we're looking at the menu in the window and [7]_____ young guy popped his head out and [8]_____ 'Come in. Come in. Best curry in Japan.' We all shuffled into this tiny room, which was darkly lit and ridiculously overdecorated – pictures, posters, musical instruments, hats, you name it. We were about to leave, but the guy was so enthusiastic, that we just couldn't. After we got the drinks in, [9]_____ Paul who asked what he'd recommend. So he goes, 'Flaming pineapple curry.' So we [10]_____ 'Yeah, that sounds good, something sweet and spicy. Can we get a couple?' We kept chatting, and then after a few minutes there's this [11]_____ weird smell in the air, kind of sweet, kind of acrid. Then smoke starts filling the room! We're panicking at this point, but then the guy walks in with a tray, and plonks it down at the table. Two pineapple halves, full of curry. Leaves ablaze and smoke billowing about the place. [12]_____ you don't forget in a hurry! [13]_____, I can't remember actually eating any of it!

LEARN TO

USE ELLIPSIS

3 A Rewrite the conversation using ellipsis.

A: Did you read this review?

B: Yes, I did. I read it this morning.

A: Have you ever seen any of his films?

B: Yes, I've seen a couple of them. They were brilliantly shot, and very atmospheric.

A: Are they always subtitled?

B: No, not always, some of them are in English.

A: Are you going to see this one?

B: I might do, but the plot sounds a bit predictable.

B ▶ 7.2 Listen and check.

8 CHOICE

VOCABULARY

IDIOMS FOR CHOICES

1 Match the sentence halves.

1 There comes a point where you just can't sit on
2 I've been weighing up the options all day, but I think I need to sleep
3 You just wouldn't believe the range. We were spoilt
4 He's got no backbone; he just goes with the line
5 I'd like my daughter to study nearby, but she's in a
6 Martin wasn't my choice, but to be honest he's the lesser of
7 I can call a taxi or just get the train. It's six of one, half a
8 I don't think Martina knows what to do. She's torn

a) for choice. But in the end, we plumped for a red one.
b) dozen of the other. It'll cost me the same.
c) between handing in her notice or putting in a complaint.
d) on it before I decide whether to take the job.
e) two evils, and might make a difference in the end.
f) quandary because her friends have opted to study abroad.
g) the fence any longer. You've got to make a decision.
h) of least resistance. I wish he'd give his own opinions.

LISTENING

2 A What are some of the key decisions that people often need to make in life? Note down your ideas.

B 8.1 You are going to listen to five short extracts where people talk about decisions they have made. For each speaker (1–5), look at the list of points in A–H below and decide what reason they give for making the decision. For questions 6–10, decide from the points in A–H what each speaker gained from their experience. Do both tasks at the same time while you listen.

A	the need to earn more		A	felt a greater sense of positivity	
B	the need for personal commitment	Speaker 1 — 1	B	gained a greater sense of control	Speaker 1 — 6
C	the need for a challenge	Speaker 2 — 2	C	made a closer bond with their community	Speaker 2 — 7
D	a job requirement	Speaker 3 — 3	D	developed new transferable skills	Speaker 3 — 8
E	to fulfil a legal obligation	Speaker 4 — 4	E	increased earnings potential	Speaker 4 — 9
F	to fulfil family obligations	Speaker 5 — 5	F	discovered a new talent	Speaker 5 — 10
G	to broaden academic understanding		G	rekindled an interest in academia	
H	a change in personal circumstances		H	achieved all their short-term goals	

C Listen again and check.

D Match the underlined words and phrases from the recording with the definitions a)–h). Read the audio script on page 69 to help you.

1 studying fell by the wayside
2 There were a lot of lucrative contracts
3 When I broached the subject of transferring
4 you just have to take that in your stride
5 a wedding would've blown our meagre savings
6 I feel more grounded
7 the kind of person who thrives on setting themselves targets
8 it turns out that I'm quite adept

a) raised for discussion
b) deal with something in a calm way
c) stopped being done
d) skilled, proficient
e) well-paid
f) stable, settled
g) inadequate, limited
h) do well in a specific situation

GRAMMAR

UNDERSTANDING COMPLEX SENTENCES

3 Write the complex sentences in the correct order. Add any commas that are needed.

1 if recent reports can be trusted / the current government / which since the early 1990s / has had a detrimental impact / has decided to end its policy / on the funding of community services

_____

_____

2 which have caused serious disruption / in recent weeks / are likely to continue / including Carlo Santi / the baggage handler strikes / into the summer months / despite the assurances / to travellers on a number of airlines / of many leading union representatives

_____

_____

3 proportion of the population / seemingly insignificant decisions / or which programme to stream next / among a significant / can create a good deal of tension / which is difficult to alleviate / like what to make for dinner

_____

_____

4 in twentieth-century photojournalism / ranging from the war photographers / such as Frank Capa / later this month / a documentary / exploring some of the key moments / to social commentators like Mike Brodie / is scheduled to be broadcast

_____

_____

4 Find examples of hidden relative clauses in the text. Then find places to add *that* or commas, and make any changes to form where needed.

Several members of the fire and rescue service, *(who were)* <u>honoured</u> for their role in rescuing the crew of a fishing vessel stranded on rocks near the remote Shiant Islands have attended an award ceremony at Edinburgh Castle. Standing outside the ceremony protesting against job losses scheduled for this month a crowd of current and former servicemen and women including representatives from the Highlands demanded they should be given greater support to carry out such dangerous work. The situation raises many questions facing rural and remote areas: Is it right we continue to centralise such services when they are so obviously essential to the communities they protect?

VOCABULARY *PLUS*

CONNOTATION

5 Underline the best alternative to compete the conversations.

1 **A:** I thought you'd made your mind up that you weren't going to take their offer?

B: I know, but they kept adding more and more incentives. In the end, I just *acquiesced/buckled/capitulated*.

2 **A:** Have you met the new guy who works in the café?

B: Sam, isn't it? Seems nice, but not exactly *articulate/garrulous/chatty*. I couldn't get a word out of him.

3 **A:** Have you thought about what you're going to make the kids for dinner?

B: I'll probably keep it pretty simple – Chloe's really *discerning/fussy/finicky* about what she eats.

4 **A:** Look at this photo! What do you think of that suit?

B: Well, it might not be the most contemporary look, but I think he's *intelligent/meticulous/well-dressed*.

5 **A:** So, we're at this café, and John's like 'Let's go Dutch.' I mean, really.

B: Sounds like him, right enough. He never offers to pay for anyone else; he's so *nit-picking/nasty/stingy*.

6 **A:** I'm really proud of her. She's done some extraordinary work in her field.

B: Absolutely, people consider her to be a pioneer. She's truly *clever/gifted/smart*.

7 **A:** They won't give up, you know.

B: You can say that again. They're *determined/headstrong/resolute* if nothing else.

8 **A:** She looks happy. Did she get top marks again?

B: Of course. She's very *proud/self-assured/conceited* and never seems to doubt her ability to succeed.

9 **A:** What did they think of your ideas, then? Any joy?

B: Well, they liked the report due to all the detail. They said it was *meticulous/nit-picking/systematic*.

10 **A:** There's someone coming from head office today to give us advice on updating our systems.

B: Oh, that'll be interesting. They are *famous/celebrated/notorious* for making change where none's needed.

VOCABULARY

WAYS OF READING

1 Complete the texts with the correct form of the words and phrases in the box.

> cast an eye over   dip into
> flick through   peruse
> plough through   pore over
> read up on   scrutinise

A

Reading? I don't seem to do as much as I used to, unless you count [1]_____ the kids' homework on a Sunday evening. In my teens though, I was an avid reader. I was really into fantasy books; you know *Game of Thrones* and the like. Some of them were massive tomes, but I'd [2]_____ a couple each month. That's the difference that parenthood brings.

B

Mainly on holiday, that's when I tend to read the most. I'll just [3]_____ a couple of the bestsellers at the airport and choose whatever piques my interest. I'm not really the biggest reader. I'll [4]_____ the same novel for about six months. My girlfriend's the opposite though, but she loves non-fiction. She's always [5]_____ politics and history. She's the same when we visit somewhere; she'll [6]_____ all the information in a museum or gallery, whereas I like to just look quickly at things.

C

I love reading all kinds of things – fiction, non-fiction. The last thing I read wasn't a book though; it was a contract for a new car. You really have to [7]_____ those things – there's so much small print. I was casually [8]_____ the first page when I found a couple of points that needed clarifying, so I'm glad I did take my time.

READING

2 A Does the writer feel that storytelling has a place in modern society? Read the article and find out.

●●● ‹ ›   🔍 🏠

We've probably all done it at some point in the past; head down, immersed and oblivious. The world around goes on and yet you are lost . . . within the pages of a book. It could even be argued that as we read our identity is subsumed by that of the narrator.

1_____

Yet increasingly, this notion of the focused or transformed reader is under siege. Storytelling and reading have gone social, meaning that instead of immersion, interaction is the USP. Over 50 percent of e-book buyers read stories on a smartphone, suggesting that disruption and interjection is very much part of the contemporary reading experience.

2_____

But as so many people are reading in this way, is it all bad? Perhaps there are advantages to this new approach which will result in a divergent creativity that, while not quite mirroring the pull of the novel, engenders something else. Reading on the internet as part of a broader community renders you a participant in a kind of shared digital consciousness.

3_____

Social reading, as the process is dubbed, is a synchronous reading practice where readers in diverse settings can simultaneously engage with a text. This often happens in real time, with readers reading, commenting on content, responding to others' comments and contributing to the development of a narrative.

4_____

These conversations occur directly inside the document or book, in its margins and even within the text itself, enabling readers to simultaneously engage with the book in real time by highlighting, underlining and discussing the content on the pages themselves. Contributions can include written text, audio and video, ensuring that the full panoply of digital delivery is realised.

5_____

It may well be that new kinds of open-ended, continuous, serial stories that transform readers into writers who are collaborating on and contributing to the story are the end result of social reading. Perhaps a new genre will be created, much in the way that the mechanised printing press allowed for the rise of the novel. Whatever the outcome, it seems that the idea of a pensive voice in your head could be displaced by a clamouring mass of creatives.

B Read the article again. Five paragraphs have been removed. Match A–F with gaps 1–5. There is one extra paragraph which you do not need.

A However, the practice shouldn't be misconstrued as just another forum for feedback, or conflated with standardised online commenting practices. True social reading isn't just an exercise in below-the-line badinage.

B According to some neuroscientists, reading on a digital device tends to shift focus towards concrete details, and away from abstract inference and higher level interpretation. They argue that digital devices inhibit deep reading.

C This is envisaged as a hive of interactivity where storyteller, reader, critic and editor are all blended into one amorphous creative mass. Instead of disappearing into a text, the reader will be able to assert themselves upon the creative process, shaping stories and the way they are read.

D Recent research would also suggest that is the case. Psychologists such as Raymond Mar, of York University, have shown via MRI scans that as we read parts of our brains light as though we were physically and mentally experiencing the same events as a protagonist.

E We are seeing the evolution of the democratisation of publishing, as there is greater access to online publishing tools and social media networks. Yet this process of democratisation doesn't necessarily herald an influx of creative works that demand our attention. Quality, it would seem, is variable in this brave new world.

F As social reading platforms and services continue to evolve, better and more refined features will be offered that will further improve this reading practice. For example, specialised commentary and real-time contributions from authors themselves or live author readings of the book taking place inside the document or book itself.

C Find words or phrases in the main part of the text that match the definitions.

1 included or absorbed into something else (para 1)
2 an abrupt aside (para 2)
3 being surrounded (para 2)
4 tending to be different (para 3)
5 occuring at the same time (para 4)
6 named (para 4)
7 extensive or impressive collection (para 5)
8 thoughtful (para 6)

GRAMMAR
PREPOSITIONAL PHRASES

3 Underline the correct alternative to complete the sentences.

1 Opposition politicians expressed their anger *at/with* the government's decision to support the ban.
2 If you decide *against/about* going out for dinner, you're welcome to eat with us.
3 I was very sceptical about their story, but after mulling it over I'm convinced *of/by* the truth of their account.
4 I'm amazed *about/by* the total ignorance shown by some so-called experts.
5 Most people are upset *about/with* the way that the situation has been handled.
6 Isn't it normal *in/for* your parents to be involved in this kind of decision?
7 It seems like they are terrified *about/of* making a suggestion that will upset anyone.
8 You needn't have any regrets *for/about* changing your mind. I would have done the same.
9 It's been increasingly difficult to believe *for/in* anything that they are publishing. online.
10 I don't feel confident *about/in* criticising her decision.

4 Circle the correct options to compete the article.

While many people will be aware ¹_____ the growing trend in readers downloading pirated e-books, and the accompanying decline ²_____ physical book sales, they might not have thought ³_____ the implications for authors and the publishing industry in general. According to recent figures from the Intellectual Property Office, 17 percent of e-books read online are pirated, which accounts for approximately 4 million books. This may be indicative ⁴_____ a mindset that anything available online should be fair game, but whatever the reasons ⁵_____ pirating material, it is affecting authors' ability to produce new material. Several prominent authors have spoken out on social media to explain the likelihood ⁶_____ ongoing series being left incomplete since publishers are forced to terminate contracts due to poor sales. At the same time, they are conscious ⁷_____ vast numbers of pirated copies being exchanged online. Creative industries have a reliance ⁸_____ engagement with their audience, yet when a title is pirated the signal given to the market is that nobody cares sufficiently to buy or borrow the material. While fans might insist ⁹_____ their devotion to a particular title or character, if this interest isn't translated into actual sales, then the writing stops. What is needed is the shift in understanding which has occurred in the film and music industries. Once fans decide ¹⁰_____ reading a pirated version, in favour of buying a book in whichever format they prefer, they are making a statement about their support for artistic expression.

	a)	b)	c)
1	at	in	of
2	for	in	with
3	against	about	around
4	of	on	in
5	about	for	with
6	of	on	for
7	at	of	on
8	about	in	on
9	at	on	with
10	against	around	about

WRITING
FOR AND AGAINST ESSAY; LEARN TO WRITE AN INTRODUCTION AND CONCLUSION

5 A Read the title and main body of a for and against essay. Which of the ideas in the notes below have been used?

> ### The only way for a modern classroom to be a meaningful learning environment is for it to promote digital skills above all others.

For

1 Addresses a range of learning styles
2 Reconfigures the learning model
3 Prepares students for future
4 Encourages greater responsibility
5 Matches current expectations

Against

1 Offers too great a distraction
2 Disparity of access out of class
3 Digital skills are not only necessity for future
4 Privacy
5 Creates an overdependence

On the one hand, when working online, students tend to pick up on transferable technological skills that will have long-term benefits. Learning to manage files, use a range of software packages and code provides a strong foundation for the demand created by the pervasive use of emergent technologies. **Furthermore**, integrating technology into education ensures that students stay engaged with the learning experience. Millennials exist in a world that is immersed in technology, so aligning the classroom with this world makes sense.

It **also** dismantles the traditional passive learning model. Students are required to interact as they navigate new processes, and teachers take on a role which involves encouraging, advising and coaching.

Conversely, it could be argued that the essential skills that are needed in the future are not technologically centred. With the growing prevalence of AI, much software-based work will be undertaken by machines. **Therefore**, skills essential for success may become creativity and critical thinking. Technology may well offer limited engagement with these important areas since many current digital learning tools are restricted in creative scope. **Despite** the falling costs of technology, it is also important to recognise that parity of access hasn't yet been achieved. **Finally**, giving precedence to digital skills creates a sense that students should use these as a default when approaching a task or problem. **However**, when students' initial response is to immediately use a tool **such as** Google to find out something, their cognitive faculties may be reduced.

B Read the introduction and conclusion paragraphs to the essay. Match each sentence 1–5 to a function a)–e).

[1]Within educational institutions students are spending an increasing amount of time developing digital skills like coding. [2]This seems to be a logical response to the pervasive nature of technology in our lives, and the demands created by the fourth industrial revolution. [3]**So**, should digital skills be promoted above all others in an attempt to address technological need?

…

[4]**In conclusion**, the importance of maintaining a flexible education that promotes critical thinking and creativity outweighs the need to deliver a purely digital approach to learning. [5]**In my view**, there needs to be a balance within education, and digital skills cannot be promoted above all others.

a) Connect with the audience by using an example relevant to them and the topic.
b) State the dilemma, either as an indirect or a rhetorical question.
c) Summarise broadly the two sides of the argument, making your position clear.
d) Comment on the example.
e) Make a clear statement of your opinion.

C Match the linking devices in bold in the texts to their function.

Contrastive: _____
Additive: _____
Exemplifying: _____
Cause-effect / Reason: _____
Other: _____

D Write a for and against essay on the following topic. Use some of the ideas from this unit to help you.

> ### The only way for a modern learning environment to be successful is to give students the choice of how, where and when they study.

VOCABULARY
WILDLIFE

1 Complete the sentences with the correct form of the words and phrases in the box.

| animals animal lover conservationist cull hunt |
| livestock lone wolf migrate pack predator prey roam |

1 Several years ago, a group of _____ campaigned to protect the wetland area from development and so they safe-guarded a number of species.
2 Supporters of the reintroduction of the elephant stress that it's important they are allowed to _____ free wherever possible.
3 As an apex _____, the European wolf plays a vital role in managing the ecosystem.
4 During the harshest winter months, large herds of deer _____ to areas where there is less snow cover.
5 If the population grows too large, the landowners organise a _____ to ensure a balance is restored.
6 One argument cited by many local farmers is that repopulating the area with wolves could threaten their _____.
7 Although I'm fond of most _____, there are a few that I'd exercise caution around.
8 It's fascinating to watch a _____ of wild dogs stalking their _____.
9 She's always been a real _____. I think she was inspired by all those documentaries she watched as a child.
10 The female group were closing in on a young buffalo when their _____ was disrupted by an opportunistic _____.

FUNCTION
GIVING OPINIONS

2 Correct the mistakes in the conversations.

1 **A:** So what are you taking on this?
B: Well, I agree in principle, but I think we need a bit more detail.
_____

2 **A:** What's your view?
B: I'm really against any shape of animal abuse. And that's how I see zoos.
_____

3 **A:** In that response I'm total with you.
B: Yes, it's a very compelling argument.
_____

4 **A:** I think that the latest legislation will go a long way to solving the problem.
B: Really? I'd show surprise if that's the case.
_____

5 **A:** Have you read the report in the paper? They reckon things'll change.
B: On facing it, it seems that'll happen, but we'll see, won't we?
_____

3 Underline the correct alternative to complete the sentences.
1 I always value your opinions, so how do you *see/view* this?
2 You get fined for littering. Why *should/will* it be any different for not recycling?
3 That's a very keen observation. No one *might/would* disagree with that.
4 To be quite honest, that doesn't surprise me in the *least/less*.
5 Well, *supposing/supposedly* so, but look at all the facts.

LEARN TO
HEDGE AN OPINION

4 A Put the underlined words in the correct order to complete the conversation.

A: Have you heard about these plans to stop prescribing antibiotics for common illnesses?
B: Yeah, there was something on the radio about it last week. Sounded quite interesting. The GP who was on said that limiting prescriptions could have a really positive effect on tackling drug-resistant superbugs.
A: Hmm. [1]Well, but no I'm expert think I it's important that any risks are properly assessed before they make a big decision like that.
B: Really? What kind of risks could there possibly be? GPs aren't exactly renowned for doing anything that will endanger patients.
A: What about kids and elderly people though? They have a tough enough time as it is without succumbing to every bug that's doing the rounds.
B: [2]feels maybe like but it's it me just dangers are always exaggerated. They're only talking about stopping dishing out pills for minor coughs and colds.
A: Well, I don't think people are ready for it yet. [3]guessing that I'm a young parent with sick kids is going to feel very differently! What if they were denied treatment?
B: Listen, I don't really think it's an issue. We've got to move with the times. Think of the inordinate expense to the health services, and what'll happen when first-line antibiotics stop being effective.
A: Well, [4]things are some there I agree with that but think that I just this is probably a step too far.

B ▶ 8.2 Listen and check.

GRAMMAR SUBJUNCTIVE

1 Circle the correct option to complete the sentences.

1 _____ what may, your job here is safe.
   a) To come   b) Come   c) Comes
2 We were anxious that everyone _____ the information at the same time.
   a) received   b) receive   c) receiving
3 If _____ be we can change our appointment for later.
   a) need   b) needed   c) needs
4 It would be better if the meeting _____ postponed until next week.
   a) were   b) will be   c) is
5 The WHO requested that the government _____ its current policy.
   a) amending   b) amend   c) will amend
6 If the tickets _____ cheaper, we would have flown fist class.
   a) had been   b) were   c) are
7 The council ruled that the restaurant _____ closed immediately.
   a) was   b) is   c) be
8 It is very important that the new information _____ taken into account.
   a) are   b) be   c) were
9 Suffice _____ we were all very surprised by the news of their break-up.
   a) say   b) says   c) to say
10 Far _____ for me to tell you what to do, but I've never liked the guy.
   a) be it   b) is it   c) it is

VOCABULARY REVIEW 1

2 Complete the texts with the words in the boxes. Two words in each box are not needed.

| chick flicks   female protagonist   flashbacks |
| formulaic plotlines   heist movies   plot twist |

A What I can't understand is the ongoing appeal of these superhero blockbusters. OK, everyone likes a bit of popcorn fodder, but the
¹_____ are so mind-numbing. A bunch of disparate people with extraordinary powers band together to save the planet – and previously hostile human inhabitants – from a vague threat. And because all the films are interconnected you get these infuriating
²_____ to what's gone on before. It's all a bit testosterone driven, too. It'd be nice to see more blockbusters with a
³_____ instead of them making up the numbers, or being the love interest. But I'm not interested in flaky ⁴_____ either – I want female characters who do more than go shopping or cry over a crush.

| bear a grudge   clicked straightaway   didn't take |
| forgive easily   meet people halfway   put a strain on |

B If there's one thing guaranteed to
⁵_____ any relationship, it's sharing a flat. When I started living here I
⁶_____ with Tanya – we'd cook meals together, watch TV, hang out. Sadly, I
⁷_____ to Clyde. I've always felt that it's important to ⁸_____, but with him there was never any compromise. And he used to drink all the milk without getting his own! Anyway, he's moving out pretty soon, so I'm happy about that. The only problem is, Tanya's going with him …

| authentic   indigenous   panoramic   soaring |
| tranquil   turbulent |

C She reckons it's probably the most
⁹_____ travel experience you can have these days. Says it's a million miles away from the all-inclusive, sun and sand deals that most people do. Something a bit different; you meet
¹⁰_____ people, and enjoy a more laid-back, ¹¹_____ existence high in the ¹²_____ peaks of Bhutan. A panacea to modern life, pure relaxation. Not for me though. When I saw the price, I nearly had a fit …

GRAMMAR ADVERBIALS

3 Rewrite the sentences using the word given.

1 You might be surpised by the news, but I'm leaving home. BELIEVE
   Difficult _____,
   I'm leaving home.
2 I found it so funny when he said he was a poet.
   AMUSEMENT
   _____,
   he told me he was a poet.
3 They were devastated when they heard you weren't coming. UTTERLY
   Your news _____
   for them.
4 We all know what went wrong. It pains us. AWARE
   We _____
   what went wrong.
5 You should definitely watch the film – it's incredible.
   THOROUGHLY
   I _____
   the film. You'll love it.
6 We had to let her go, although we were reluctant.
   RELUCTANCE
   _____
   we let her go.

VOCABULARY PLUS ADVERB-ADJECTIVE COLLOCATIONS

4 Underline the correct alternatives.

1 They were *bitterly/hopelessly* disappointed not to win a prize.

2 Did you see those shoes? *Predominantly/Prohibitively* expensive, but so tempting.

3 Doctor Moore? Oh yes, he's *greatly/fundamentally* admired in the profession.

4 I think we should fly; it's *vitally/infinitely* preferable to taking the train.

5 Have you met his sister? She's lovely, but *painfully/obviously* shy.

6 It's *greatly/highly* unlikely that you'll get there on time.

7 Do you know him? He seems *vaguely/clearly* familiar.

8 I *perfectly/distinctly* remember you locking the door before we left.

9 It's *utterly/vitally* important that I speak to someone in authority.

10 I think that the problem is *inextricably/unexpectedly* linked to childhood trauma.

FUNCTION TELLING ANECDOTES

5 Complete the conversations with the words and phrases in the box.

| funny I think it was It was one of those things |
| some strange was like were like |
| you know what I mean |

1 **A:** Ah, mate! What a night! We hit downtown and partied hard.
B: _____, nobody told me. I wasn't invited!

2 **A:** So, tell me, heard any gossip from the party?
B: Well, someone, Sarah, maybe? _____ Sarah, poured her drink over this guy's head.

3 **A:** What happened to you?
B: There I was, minding my own business, and _____ bloke punched me!

4 **A:** _____. Why would anyone do that?
B: Well, I did ask his girlfriend for her phone number.

5 **A:** So, I'm halfway up the ladder, trying to look brave, _____?
B: Ha,ha, bet you were petrified. What happened then?

6 **A:** So, I _____, there's no way you can wear that!
B: Yeah, yeah, and we _____ nah, you look great, put it on!

7 **A:** Did he do the karaoke in the end?
B: Oh yeah. _____ I won't forget in a hurry.

VOCABULARY REVIEW 2

6 Complete the text with the words and phrases in the box.

| cull   dip into   migrate   pack   pore over |
| scrutinise   sit on the fence   spoilt for choice |
| torn between   weighing up the options |

As a new generation of poets [1]_____ from traditional publishing models, readers are [2]_____. New and engaging works are available on Instagram and Tumblr, ensuring that social media helps bring the medium to the literary fore. The more creative poets distinguish themselves from the [3]_____ by embedding video, music and newsfeeds into their material. These changes return the medium to the everyday. People that may have never considered taking the time to [4]_____ a book of poetry will now actively seek it out. Fans love to [5]_____ new texts, offering comment and creating a community of dedicated readers. And social media publishing circumvents an industry which historically lacks diversity, failing to give many poets a voice. [6]_____ silence and compromise, they have chosen their own route to publication. However, there is one issue I simply can't [7]_____ about. Traditional filters on quality are lost, allowing an abundance of mediocrity. If you take time to [8]_____ many internet poets in great detail, they offer a string of clichés, albeit offset with some artistic flair. Perhaps the burgeoning genre could do with a [9]_____ to ensure only the strongest poets thrive, but [10]_____ that would seem counter-productive in a developing art form that celebrates access and engagement.

GRAMMAR UNDERSTANDING COMPLEX SENTENCES

7 Rewrite the notes into one sentence using all you know about building complex sentences. Don't use relative pronouns. Start with 'According to …'.

Numerous studies looked at what popular and commercially successful films have in common.

The studies focused on high-impact releases, i.e. films which are:
• designed to be viewed on the largest screens available
• marketed heavily in advance of release
• aren't unduly affected by poor press reviews

These studies showed that high-impact releases:
• tend to be focused on a limited range of genre (e.g. heist movies, chick flicks)
• are more likely to feature recognised A-listers
• tend to be referenced visually or in dialogue by other films

VOCABULARY PLUS CONNOTATION

8 Complete the pairs of sentences with the correct word or phrase.

1 articulate / garrulous
- **a)** She's one of the most _____ people I've ever met. She can put herself across very well.
- **b)** He's a nice enough person, but a bit _____ – he never really knows when to keep quiet.

2 capitulated / buckled
- **a)** The team played well for the first twenty minutes, but finally _____ under pressure.
- **b)** Emerson eventually _____ when Dryer had him in checkmate. It was a fascinating chess tournament.

3 famous / celebrated
- **a)** She's one of Bollywood's most _____ actors, with a slew of awards to her name.
- **b)** You really ought to visit this most _____ example of Moorish architecture in the region.

4 nit-picking / systematic
- **a)** They are always _____ over tiny details. I'm not sure if we'll ever finish the report.
- **b)** Police organised a _____ search of the surrounding area, but to no avail.

5 self-assured / proud
- **a)** My niece is a _____ teenager who always seems to know best.
- **b)** She's the _____ owner of a beautifully reconditioned Norton motorbike.

6 determined / resolute
- **a)** A political giant, he was _____ in his fight for equality.
- **b)** I'm _____ to be heard. This campaign is not going to end.

7 smart / well-dressed
- **a)** Oh, you look _____! Are you going somewhere nice for dinner?
- **b)** There's a tall, _____ young man waiting at the door. Can't be for you, can it?

8 mean / nasty
- **a)** Some of the kids have been quite _____ and not let anyone play with them.
- **b)** She's got a _____ temper. You want to watch you don't upset her.

9 picky / discerning
- **a)** It's the kind of place that attracts an exceptionally _____ clientele.
- **b)** They are so _____ about what to eat.

10 gifted / smart
- **a)** So, you think you're _____, do you? Answer this then.
- **b)** Katie's daughter is incredibly _____. She's already been selected for the junior choir.

GRAMMAR PREPOSITIONAL PHRASES

9 Complete the texts with the correct prepositions.

A To be totally honest, I've been aware [1]_____ the marked decline [2]_____ quality for years. Libraries used to be somewhere that offered a bit of sanctuary, now they will insist [3]_____ making everything interactive and appealing to youth. I can understand their reasons [4]_____ wanting to get more people using the facility, but surely this over-reliance [5]_____ technology is going a bit far. It's not a 'digital hub', it's a library! I'm conscious [6]_____ the fact that this'll make me sound old-fashioned, but what's wrong with upholding traditional values? I think it's indicative [7]_____ a wider policy to get rid of physical spaces that the community can use. The likehood [8]_____ this place being open next year is minimal.

B Some people are just terrified [9]_____ change, if you ask me. I mean, it's totally normal [10]_____ other services to move with the times, so why not libraries, too? Sadly a few of our older patrons are convinced [11]_____ the fact that we're getting mothballed by the council. That's definitely not the case. I've been amazed [12]_____ some of the vitriol my staff have had to face. I know when people are upset [13]_____ something they tend to be quite frank, but there's no need for aggression. We had thought [14]_____ holding an open day to discuss some of the main issues, but I think that could do more harm than good. We have decided [15]_____ installing quite so many computer terminals though, following feedback. It's important that students don't develop too great a reliance [16]_____ the web for their assignments.

FUNCTION GIVING OPINIONS

10 A Put the underlined words in the correct order.

- **a)** your / what's / view?
- **b)** surprised / really / be / I'd / that's / case / if / the.
- **c)** face / on / it / the / of, it seems possible. It's not well-attended.
- **d)** respect / that / I'm / you / totally / in / with.
- **e)** what's / on / this / your / take / so?

B Complete the conversations with the sentences from Exercise 10A.

1 A: _____
   B: Well, to be honest I find it totally unacceptable.

2 A: _____
   B: My view? I'm all for it, actually.

3 A: They are bound to impeach him, for sure.
   B: _____

4 A: _____
   B: Yes, you can't really argue against that, can you?

5 A: Do you think they'll decide to close the school?
   B: _____

CHECK

Circle the correct option to complete the sentences.

1 There was an unexpected _____ that had the audience reeling.
   a) flashback   b) plotline   c) plot twist

2 I think I've seen this before. The _____, she's not well-known, is she?
   a) A-lister   b) female protagonist
   c) supporting cast

3 I _____ rather you didn't do that.
   a) could   b) should   c) would

4 It has _____ said he get's things done quickly, doesn't he?
   a) be   b) to be   c) been

5 He requested his ashes _____ scattered on this beach.
   a) are   b) were   c) be

6 I'm not one to _____ a grudge. Come on, give me a hug.
   a) strain   b) bear   c) stable

7 We're _____ friendly terms these days, at least.
   a) on   b) of   c) in

8 I really didn't take _____ him when we first met.
   a) from   b) with   c) to

9 They've made a _____ promising start to the match.
   a) fair   b) fairly   c) widely

10 They were _____ knowledgable about the topic but could do with updating their research.
   a) relatively   b) very   c) really

11 Her class this term is _____ female.
   a) bitterly   b) infinitely   c) predominantly

12 He's _____ inadequate for the task in hand.
   a) helplessly   b) hopelessly   c) hopefully

13 We met people from one of the three _____ tribes on the island.
   a) authentic   b) opulent   c) indigenous

14 They lived here during the revolution. _____ times, those were.
   a) Legendary   b) Turbulent   c) Soaring

15 I asked her on a date and she _____ like, 'Really? No, chance.'
   a) were   b) be   c) was

16 The trouble with you is that you've been spoilt for _____.
   a) choice   b) choose   c) choices

17 Well. I'm not sold on it, but it's the lesser of two _____.
   a) fences   b) paths   c) evils

18 Don't decide now, just sleep _____ it.
   a) with   b) on   c) over

19 Oh, your little boy is ever so _____. Three, isn't he?
   a) articulate   b) chatty   c) garrulous

20 It says here he was one of America's most _____ and violent gangsters.
   a) celebrated   b) famous   c) notorious

21 Could you _____ over this? I don't want to make any mistakes.
   a) cast an eye   b) flick through   c) read up on

22 The guy at border control really _____ my paperwork.
   a) perused   b) dipped into   c) scrutinised

23 They decided _____ going in the end as it was so expensive.
   a) for   b) against   c) with

24 I'm just petrified _____ making some kind of faux pas.
   a) of   b) about   c) in

25 The decline _____ fish stocks has worried environmentalists.
   a) of   b) on   c) in

26 Thousands of zebra _____ through the valley each summer.
   a) hunt   b) pack   c) migrate

27 Farmers are concerned about the ill-health of their _____.
   a) prey   b) livestock   c) animals

28 A well-known _____, he was awarded for his work protecting dolphins.
   a) predator   b) animal lover   c) conservationist

29 How do you _____ this issue?
   a) see   b) view   c) find

30 I think that the policy will go a long _____ to solving the problem.
   a) route   b) path   c) way

RESULT   /30

UNIT 1   Recording 1

We live in a time of big challenges, but also of huge opportunities. As emergent technologies continue to improve, a new generation of designers, innovators and pioneers is addressing the pressing issues of the day through game-changing technology.

Talib Alhinai is one such pioneer. Working in the field of aerial robotics, he has designed a prototype for a flying robot which can be used to build structures. Given the right development, these autonomous flying robots could have a profound effect on both construction and space travel. The devices, very similar to drones, are capable of printing structures in 3D while in flight. The potential applications for the technology include disaster relief, where drones could work together to 3D print temporary shelters using local materials. Within more standard construction, the drones could be assigned tasks currently deemed too dangerous for human builders, thereby reducing the incidence of workplace accidents. And in the future, the technology may be used to construct habitats when colonising other planets. Conventional wisdom says that the risks of colonising somewhere like Mars are too great, but Alhinai's design could provide a solution which would rewrite the rulebook.

Sometimes, the need for innovation can be closer to home. For example, in our kitchens. Approximately one third of the food products produced for mass consumption worldwide, that's 1.3 billion tons, is disposed of without being consumed. One reason is that the expiry date printed on food labels discourages consumers from buying products, and this has a direct economic impact on producers, who end up throwing away 16 percent of their stock before it has actually gone bad. Solveiga Pakštaitė developed Mimica Touch to address that issue. Mimica Touch is a multilayer food label, comprised of a layer of plastic, followed by a layer of gelatin, another layer of plastic with protuberances and a final, smooth layer of plastic. As the food changes in chemical composition, the gelatin reacts. While the label remains smooth to the touch, the food product within is still good, and when bumps become detectable this indicates that the food product has gone bad. This could be a major breakthrough in food sustainability, and mean that the days of throwing out still-fresh produce could be over.

Another innovator with an eye on environmental sustainability is materials scientist Sam Stranks. He and a team based at MIT have been developing lightweight, efficient and malleable solar conductors from a man-made, cost-effective substance known as perovskite. The material is made from two cheap and readily abundant salts which are mixed to make an ink that can be pressed into very thin film. Unlike conventional solar panels, the resulting conductors will be so light that they can easily be transported into areas of the developing world which are currently energy deficient. Akin to Alhinai's drones, they can be rapidly deployed to provide aid in disaster zones. Furthermore, perovskite can be tinted to allow this source of renewable energy to have an aesthetic and functional appeal. Future skyscrapers could be coated in varying hues of perovskite, offering an attractive integration of solar cell technology into architectural projects. It is hoped that this application encourages considerable investment into a substance that could transform our environment for good.

UNIT 1   Recording 2

Another illustration of this, is the number of people between the ages of eighteen and twenty-five who applied for tax relief, but who, as it happened, hadn't paid any tax.

UNIT 1   Recording 3

Does it really matter whether businesses have a social agenda, as long as they are benefiting the economy? Many people may believe that, in an increasingly globalised world, we should be more philanthropic, that is, caring. However, there's no point in speaking of doing this, if nobody's quality of life improves, is there?

UNIT 2   Recording 1

Extract 1

So, I've been doing this pottery course at a local community centre for the past few months. It's just a small group of us at the moment – when we started, there were quite a number of participants, but over time numbers have dwindled. Not that that's a bad thing – it certainly means that I've had more opportunity to grill the instructor, Robin, about different techniques. As a free-time activity it's not exactly cheap, but then I think when you take into account the materials that are required each week, and the cost of firing pots, it feels about right. One drawback is that a community centre ought to be hosting courses that are readily within the budget of people living in the area. Having said that, seniors and the unemployed are subsidised. One thing I'd certainly take from it is that you're not going to become accomplished overnight. I've probably thrown more bad pots than good – but how else are you going to learn? The instructors are keen to help, but it's about trial and error really. Provided that you are willing to keep it up.

Extract 2

There are times when I feel you're derided for pointing out the importance of creative expression. I know that the emphasis for everyone is numeracy and literacy – this current obsession with assessment has done that. But it's quite naïve to think that learning to play the guitar, or paint or … or draw, doesn't have any inherent value as part of a mainstream curriculum. It wasn't that long ago that nearly everyone would have some access to the arts at school. I wouldn't want to cast aspersions on head teachers, because they're just trying to get on with limited resources. But the government is totally misguided in cutting back on itinerant teachers who offer art or music lessons. You've got to think about education holistically – not everyone's going to be an academic success, but they may well show creative talents. I'm frustrated that kids have such limited access to my lessons. I get a big buzz when I first get the chance to play with teenagers who may never have picked up an instrument. So often they are tentative to begin with, but then really take to it. All the attitude drops away, and they just start having fun. Surely that's a valuable learning experience?

UNIT 2   Recording 2

I = Interviewer   A = Andrea

I: So, Andrea, you're a graduate, and up until recently had been undergoing teacher training. I understand that after some deliberation you've chosen not to pursue that career. Can you give us a bit of an insight into some of the challenges you see in the profession? I mean, what informed your decision?

A: Well, if you look at the statistics, it's fairly obvious that the current workload is problematic for teachers here in the UK.

I: Could you elaborate on that? Many listeners will assume that teachers have a pretty good deal, in terms of paid holidays, working conditions …

A: Well, it's interesting that you mention working conditions. I think it's important that we see teaching as a bit more than classroom-focused time. I think there's too great an emphasis on that, and little on seeing the profession as a place where ongoing intellectual development is encouraged. That's not mirrored elsewhere.

I: How so?

A: Well, if you look at the OECD statistics, you'll soon see that teachers in England spend far more time teaching than their peers globally. I think it's

817 hours compared to an average of 704 hours.

I: And what kind of difference does that make to teaching?

A: Well, a lot has to do with opportunities to develop new ideas or resources, or even deepening knowledge of subject matter. In Japan, secondary teachers spend 32 percent of their time at work in the classroom. That's 610 hours a year. For the rest of that time they have opportunities for professional development …

I: And you think that's lacking here in the UK?

A: I think that the profession is certainly less intellectually attractive to graduates. People want to take on a role that will develop over time. You can't have a specialisation if you aren't given the opportunity to explore your field, and learn, too.

I: But don't teachers already get professional development time?

A: I think that what tends to happen is that any time out of the classroom is quickly taken up with administrative tasks.

I: And what would you prefer to see?

A: Well, good teaching, and as an extension good education, is all about collaboration and communication. If teachers could spend more time working with colleagues, observing other teachers' classrooms, preparing materials collectively, and even working with parents, that would make a tremendous difference to the role.

I: Does that happen elsewhere?

A: Well, it's certainly something that seems to go on in the highest performing education systems – Japan, South Korea, Finland. Teachers have more time to engage with one another and to build better working practices.

I: Are there any other areas that you feel need to be addressed? To make the profession more attractive for graduates?

A: Alongside making it intellectually attractive, it has to be financially rewarding, too. Sadly, teaching salaries have been declining in real terms for some time.

UNIT 2 Recording 3

1

A: So, our task today is to discuss creative approaches to educational improvement. Who'd like to kick this one off? Sally?

B: Yeah, sure. Well, I've been looking at some of the ways attainment is being addressed at primary levels. Rather than traditional testing

forms, students are being offered the opportunity to prepare task-focused work which highlights their learning.

A: Could you elaborate on that?

B: Well, the idea is that they work together to make or develop something which can show teachers what they've picked up during the academic year.

2

A: Tony, you mentioned schools specialising in one particular medium. Could you explore that further?

B: Sure, there are situations where schools have developed partnerships with professionals in the creative industries to push a broader skills base. For instance, collaborating with a local radio station or gallery.

A: I can imagine that working. Students could get a lot out of that.

B: Yeah, and it ties into a lot of subject areas – the arts, communication, ITC …

UNIT 2 Recording 4

1

A: Did you want to add anything, Kate?

B: Yes, actually, I was wondering if you'd read the report on forest schools.

2

A: The main reason that the attainment gap is growing is lack of training.

B: Can I make a comment about that?

3

A: Substantially less is spent on teacher training than in the past.

B: I think we might be digressing …

4

A: Can I just wrap up what I was saying?

B: OK, but can you make it a quick point?

5

A: Well, I'm not convinced myself, I think …

B: Can we just hear what Paul wanted to say?

6

A: Look, there's a video about it online. I'll show you …

B: We're pressed for time, so let's move on.

UNIT 3 Recording 1

1 I've always been interested in doing something in the field, but it's increasingly challenging to find real, meaningful work experience when 'internship' is often just a euphemism for office dogsbody. I'm not averse to hard work, but it certainly has to be something that is going to benefit me in the long run. This post has that. There's a tremendous amount to be

learnt from the staff here, who are all so supportive. They've got a positive mindset, which I think filters down from the management's ethos. That approach has given me the kind of boost I needed. I've got a renewed sense of optimism in what I do.

2 Travel time was probably one of the most important criteria for me. It's easy to say that you're flexible, but when you're commuting several hours a day for an unpaid internship, it's not cost-effective. I need as much as I can just to keep afloat, living here. When I saw this post, I was ecstatic. Within walking distance of the college, so I can keep up with my studies and make tutorials when I need to. So far, the balance between academia and work has been manageable. There are a couple of other interns with similar research goals, too. It's been good to make a connection with them. I suppose it's allowed me to branch out a bit.

3 This has been a real eye-opener for me. The pace is relentless, and the expectation to succeed is constantly high. It can be stressful, especially as so much of what you do is results driven, but it's given me such a buzz and I know it's where I want to be career-wise. You need to understand the markets from a global perspective, and that's where they are particularly strong here, especially as they operate in so many different places. I've learnt a lot about working across time zones and some of the nuances of different working cultures. That's bound to help, going forward. If they offered me a permanent post here tomorrow, I doubt I'd take it. But I do know that it's given me a taste for this kind of work.

4 I was initially looking for something that tied in with my degree, but that was proving pretty difficult. Fortunately, a friend of mine saw this post advertised and said I should consider it. I'm glad I did. They are doing some incredibly innovative things in terms of research and development. It's beyond anything I've read about elsewhere. It's rewarding to be in a place where people aren't risk averse, and want to be at the forefront of change. The next project is focusing on the use of microprocessors in wearable technology. That is something I've considered while studying, so it'll be interesting to test some assumptions.

5 I'd been studying abroad on an exchange when this cropped up. One of the tutors had been instrumental in getting the project up and running. I think it's in its fourth year now. It's hard to get a post on something like this, so I've been lucky. There are obvious challenges, with cultural barriers and colleagues occasionally having unrealistic expectations of my abilities. But all in all, working with wildlife is something you don't get to do very often. Here on the reserve things can be tough, but you work through it. I think that it makes you value the importance of being part of something bigger.

UNIT 3   Recording 2

A: So, Minister, according to the front page of today's papers, you claimed, 'Students get more than their fair share of government funds.' Would you care to elaborate on that?

B: Well, before we begin, I'd like to say that quote was taken out of context. I'm a firm supporter of extending free tuition where possible.

A: So, can you explain your party's plans to cut bursaries for students from low-income backgrounds?

B: Well, what we have to take into account is that there are many reasons for reassessing the education budget. Especially with regards to tertiary education.

A: Do you feel that perhaps they are unworthy of your investment?

B: Before I answer that, let me just add to what I was saying. The state of the public finances left by the last government has meant we have to look across the board at spending decisions.

A: So, you've not got enough money?

B: Listen, all I'm saying is that there's a problem with continuing some of the policies that we inherited. However, we're committed to providing affordable solutions.

A: By reducing education spending and allowing tuition fees to go uncapped?

B: OK, let me put it into perspective. There are many other countries where this is happening. We need a more competitive model.

UNIT 4   Recording 1

As part of a social species, we are strongly influenced by the example of others – from following fashions to sharing likes, subscribing to similar mindsets is a fundamental part of our everyday lives. Our interests and even our goals are frequently adopted from those around us without conscious thought. In their most nascent form, role models are our parents and close family. But as we grow and are exposed to the wider world, the opportunity for influence from beyond this unit becomes more prevalent. As social learning theory would have it, good role models are essential to ensuring that children and young adults encode positive traits and behaviours. The desire

to emulate, and be rewarded for this, is strong. Continued positive modelling, which is copied and rewarded, leads to a sense of reinforcement. And that is when a powerful role model can have a profound effect on long-term attitudes and aspirations.

Culturally, we are faced with a broader range of prospective role models than ever before – especially as we reside in an age where online media thrives on the fascination for constant updates of celebrity achievement or excess. Some of these role models are positive – achieving success in the face of adversity, or shaping their industries with consummate ease. Others less so. And the dividing lines are often not so clear-cut. Historically, a statesman or woman was a trusted role model; someone who could be looked upon to assess, evaluate and respond to all manner of crises in a level-headed fashion. Nowadays, that image is somewhat out of kilter. Athletes offered inspiration for those who showed a desire for sporting success. Then doping scandals toppled some of our idols and tarnished both reputations and medals.

But does any of that matter? Could ostensibly negative role models, who often exhibit self-destructive or damaging behaviours, actually offer some semblance of influence that results in positive outcomes? Interestingly enough, research into motivation suggests that it can, and does. Evidently, we use positive and negative role models in differing ways, depending on what we are hoping to achieve or avoid. When we want to achieve a goal, say passing an exam, we tend to select role models who have a positive attitude towards learning and attainment. And we seek to emulate their actions. If this aspiration is reframed as a fear of failure, then we tend to identify negative role models – those who haven't put in the effort – and motivate ourselves by attempting to avoid reproducing their bad behaviour. We become driven to distance ourselves from their inability to achieve.

However, there is compelling evidence that role models who are immediately accessible, rather than distant idols placed on a pedestal, are far better for our mental well-being. According to cutting-edge neurobiological studies, a good deal of what we do is dependent upon mirror neurons. When we see someone undergo an action, an involuntary and automatic neural mechanism within the brain allows us to copy this and show empathy or understanding. These mirror neurons provide a biological basis for imitation – and this suggests that having role models who are within your close environment may be more efficacious than those held in high regard, but at a distance.

UNIT 4   Recording 2

1   Not only is the car economical, it's stylish, too.
2   Who wouldn't want a deal like that?
3   Under pressure stay cool, calm and collected.
4   To be successful, you need to work hard and play harder.
5   'We love being part of the team. Join us.'
6   It's a dog eat dog world here.

UNIT 4   Recording 3

1   Despite the obvious pressures, he's a great presenter; he's self-confident, successful and succinct.
2   I found him generous and genuine although a little juvenile in character.
3   She's incredibly patient and pertinent without being overly persuasive. That's a good thing.
4   I liked what they had to say; they were confident, compelling and concise.
5   The information we received was both critical and credible.
6   I'm not overly fond of your boss; he's proud, pushy and pompous.
7   What a lovely old bloke – articulate, urbane and earnest.

UNIT 5   Recording 1

P = Presenter   C = Charlotte de Witte
L = Luke Slater

P: The microbiome, just another health fad? A bit of scientific jargon to feed the need for knowledge in our body-conscious zeitgeist? Here to discuss this are two researchers from the university biology department, Charlotte de Witte and Luke Slater. So, Charlotte, is the microbiome such a big deal?

C: Well, yes, it's certainly a term which is growing in currency, but I think that 'fad' is a bit of a pejorative. Your microbiome technically refers to the genetic map of all the microbes that inhabit a human body. In popular discourse, that technical meaning has been conflated with a broader definition to refer to the collection of microbes in general. It is a fascinating area of study, and one which could provide a rich seam of solutions to common ailments. Luke?

L: I'd thoroughly concur with that. We're looking at an area of science still very much in its infancy, so castigating it for making headline news is a bit unfair. It wasn't until 2007 that the initial Human Microbiome Project began, by taking samples from roughly 300 volunteers. That came to an end in 2013, so it was short lived as studies go, but the data gathered was truly remarkable in those intervening years. That all contributed to the widely accepted idea that many varieties of bacteria in our lower intestine have a considerable impact on our general health.

C: And the technology for sequencing bacteria is fine-tuning research all the time. Recent studies have provided concrete evidence that microbial groupings carry out specific jobs within the body. Some groups found in the mouth help break down sugars and nitrates, while others synthesise vitamin B. There are others which break down short-chain fatty acids from typically high-fibre foods like fruit and vegetables.

P: So what sort of research is likely to get the most support?

L: Something that the scientific community is getting fired up about is studies into the interaction patterns between microbial groups. There seems to be a certain amount of symbiosis which, if we understand better, can be used to help address issues such as obesity, diabetes, even depression. I think educating the public about maintaining a healthy microbiome is key to this, though. Charlotte?

C: I agree. For some people there's this assumption that the microbiome you have is stable, and you can do little to change it. That isn't the case at all. Lots of factors lead to their biodiversity – what you eat, drink, the air you breathe, even exercise. In dietary terms, prebiotics are essential. Fermented foods, like sauerkraut and kimchi, contain these in high numbers. They'll help regulate a lot of the biological processes in digestion to ensure you get the most nutrition from your intake, and burn off excess calories.

P: Right, so the microbiome is a way to approach dieting?

L: It's not just about weight loss though, as important as that is. Gut bacteria is a fundamental building-block in immune system regulation. Changing the balance of your microbiome can address autoimmune and allergic diseases like asthma or eczema. We're exploring a whole range of different areas where the health of our gut can make profound differences to general health. People can make conscious decisions to affect this.

C: Absolutely. A study being conducted here is still in an inchoate stage, but early indications are that a co-abundance of bacteria and fungi are greater in volunteers with low-fat diets. As yet we haven't drawn any conclusions, but there's a strong enough correlation to suggest a number of health conditions could be addressed just by limiting fat intake.

UNIT 5   Recording 2

A: So, I hear that you've been following a Paleo diet recently. What's that all about then? Isn't it loading up on protein, and getting all prehistoric? What's the appeal of eating like a caveman?

B: It's not just about eating meat, there's a bit more to it than that. It's more to do with excluding or avoiding anything that is processed – and there's no dairy, added salt or sugar. You only eat things Paleolithic people would have had, about 10,000 years ago …

A: Sounds like it's very limiting. Why would you want to put yourself through something like that?

B: Well, apart from the weight loss, it does have proven benefits for increasing energy levels. It's a pretty healthy option, overall.

A: Really? I would have thought that you'd be missing out on all the vitamins and minerals from dairy stuff.

B: Well, you get plenty of those from fresh fruit and nuts. And seafood. That's a big part of the diet. I really do think Paleo is the way forward.

A: Well, if you ask me, it sounds like a fad. I'm sure that modern food production can't be all that bad. And aren't there really valuable nutrients in wheat products? You can't be eating any of those.

B: I don't know if you've tried it, but you can get lots of nutrients from raw seaweed. It's a bit tricky to track down, but I've got a tub of stuff from the local beach.

A: No thanks, I think I'll stick to my usual 21st-century snacks.

B: Don't be so dismissive. The advantage of something like this is you'll lose weight quickly, and feel more energised.

A: And end up with skin like a cavewoman. Great! What I've found really works for me is a nice pasta salad!

UNIT 6   Recording 1

I = Interviewer   A = Anja

I: So, Anja, you've been working in your industry for the best part of a decade now. What would you say some of the main challenges are?

A: Well, it can be incredibly demanding, as there's so much at stake. Both professionally and financially. If I do my job well, then there's the obvious opportunity that what we've made will gain critical acclaim, possibly awards. Get it wrong, and the most profound drama becomes a laugh-out-loud comedy.

I: Are there any areas you particularly have to be watchful of?

A: Sure, lots of foreign-language movies these days are contemporary stories – we've moved on from your typical historical costume dramas.

I: And how does that change things?

A: Well, there's a lot more slang used and that never really translates directly. You need to use a lot of creativity with subtitles, otherwise the audience will just end up confused. I suppose the ultimate goal is to convey the same idea, so you try to find an approximation of that.

I: I guess that swearing can be a problem, too.

A: Yeah. Profane language is pretty much universal, but there are definite differences between cultures. Something that might shock an audience in the UK or US could be fairly commonplace in other parts of the world. Or vice versa. You have to be aware of the probable impact of the words, but, overall, you have to think really carefully about what the screenwriter and director want to express in a scene.

I: And, are there any technical challenges?

A: Yes, there's a lot more going on than most members of your audience will have considered.

I: Such as?

A: Well, a standard subtitle contains a maximum of thirty-five characters per line, including spaces and punctuation. And you are allowed a maximum of two lines on screen at one time. The average viewer reads that in about six seconds, but your subtitle can't run over a change of scene.

I: That sounds tricky!

A: It certainly is. Especially when you need to synchronise as much as possible with the audio track. And not block anything important on screen. There's also the fact that each subtitle has to have line breaks that make it easy for viewers to read at speed. Sometimes you find yourself spending hours over even the smallest exchange.

I: Is there anything that you find more difficult than anything else?

A: Gestures. I think that they are tough for all translators, no matter which area of the industry you are involved in. There's an intercultural aspect to it. Across countries and cultures, there are subtle distinctions in meaning so a translator really needs to be on top of that. But the biggest challenge is when you are subtitling something, and a gesture is essential to explaining the plot.

I: So, would you recommend your job to someone interested in languages?

A: Oh, absolutely. It's not an easy job, as I mentioned, but a well-translated film can have such an emotional impact on audiences that it's a privilege to be able to do it. And in terms of remuneration, it's pretty good, so that's a bonus factor, too.

UNIT 6 Recording 2

1 You'd think I'd be accustomed to it by now, I mean, I've been living here since the late 90s. It's not like Italy is a million miles away, and we do have a lot of things in common. But I just can't get used to piling all my food on to one plate. Friends always think it's so funny when I ask for a side dish so I can separate my meat and vegetables. It's just what I'm used to, though. And don't get me started on pasta. People here don't really seem to get it that penne and pesto don't go together …

2 When it first happened I found it a completely alien experience. I mean, people back home tend to pay you little attention, but here was an entire floor of staff all calling out 'irrashaimase'. One after another, like a wave. But the weird thing was most of them didn't even look up from stocking shelves, or whatever else they were doing. I didn't know at the time, but it's a given that when a new customer comes in they should be welcomed to the store. It certainly makes for an interesting experience when you are in one of those huge supermarkets downtown.

3 I come from London, so I am used to people being a bit stand-offish. Generally, when you go out you're unlikely to get into a conversation with anyone. It's all a bit heads-down. I suppose that's just the nature of city life. Out here everything is a bit more laid-back. People tend to know one another, and if they don't, they'll most likely have a mutual friend in common. The norm is to help each other out if you possibly can. I still remember being taken aback when I asked a shopkeeper for directions. He walked out of his place with me, down the road and to the station, so I'd get there safely. I don't even think he bothered to lock up!

UNIT 6 Recording 3

1

A: I read an online article that says British tourists aren't welcome in the city anymore.

B: I always wonder about these things, you know, what's the evidence?

2

A: There's a huge problem with online bullying in high schools.

B: I still wonder if it's really that common. I've never heard of it happening.

3

A: Asian people tend to be the most reluctant to speak at meetings, don't they?

B: I've heard that, but it sounds like a stereotype. I know a lot of very talkative Japanese people.

4

A: Women are generally much better at listening to others than men.

B: Do you really think it's always the case? It's a pretty sweeping statement.

5

A: They'll be really offended if you don't eat what they offer you.

B: Somehow I doubt it's generally true. People tend to be aware that not everyone has the same taste.

UNIT 7 Recording 1

P = Presenter   T = Tony   E = Emma

P: Despite changing consumption patterns, as viewers switch from the big screen to streaming, the global film industry is still in pretty good financial health. So, opinions on bankable cinematic content are gold dust. Here to discuss how tastes are shaped are Tony Law and Emma Burton, both independent film journalists. So, Tony, isn't it the director who calls the shots?

T: Well, that's certainly the conventional view, but I'd say it's somewhat misguided to presume that there's only one person at the helm deciding on the narrative arc. Studios, stars, and perhaps more importantly of late, test audiences play a fundamental role in deciding what hits our screens. Wouldn't you agree, Emma?

E: Absolutely. Film-makers are notoriously divided on the value of test screenings, but the studios are giving them a lot more credence. And interestingly the process has become much more scientific of late. Gone are the days when errant data from biased questionnaires would confound matters. It's all about neurocinematics, and biometric data.

T: Yeah, I think that incorporating more scientific approaches has gone some way to assuage fears that key scenes changed due to test screening responses might flop when playing to paying audiences. With more precise ways to gauge interest levels and emotional investment, you're going to have more faith in your final product.

P: So, can you explain what some of the processes are?

E: Sure. In many ways test screenings haven't particularly changed over the last few decades; it's just how the audiences are assessed that's different. So it's important to get a fair representation of target demographics, and, assuming export value is important to you, ethnicity. In the past, you would have had a list of questions, and a focus group to discuss themes. Now, you're more likely to be given a wearable device to pick up pulse, skin temperature, electrodermal activity, motion. All of that data can be analysed to assess the efficacy of what's going on, on screen.

T: Exactly. For film-makers and studios that kind of biometric data is a game-changer. There's no more over-reliance on subjectivity, or even the vagaries of fashion. Physical responses to certain scenes or potential endings can help determine the structure of a film much more accurately. You can work out where fight-or-flight responses are stimulated, at which points viewers are literally transfixed, and how effective those shock-inducing jump cuts actually are.

E: That's right. And there's also a wealth of data coming from MRI scans. They take images of the cerebral cortex and can show whether your audience is showing synchronous activity during viewing. The more synchronous the audience brains are, the more they are all focusing on the same content. You've got their attention. And a rapt audience is more engaged, and likely to view the film positively.

P: Really, so is technology shaping our cultural content?

T: That is one area that worries me, to be honest. I'm all for getting an accurate view of cinematic success, but what I wouldn't want to see is more homogenised content that lacks subtlety or focuses solely on high-impact physical responses. Cinema is art, and art should be more nuanced, don't you think? I'd say that …

UNIT 7 Recording 2

A: Read this review?

B: Yes, this morning.

A: Ever seen his films?

B: Yes, a couple. Brilliantly shot, very atmospheric.

A: Always subtitled?

B: Not always. Some are in English.

A: Going to see this one?

B: Might do. Plot sounds a bit predictable.

UNIT 8 Recording 1

1 As a child I spent veritable hours with my head in a book, pouring over facts and figures and scouring the indexes for curious customs from far-flung places. I was quite obsessed with anything arcane and a bit unsettling … I suppose a lot of little boys are. But as I grew older, work and family took over and studying fell by the wayside. But retirement meant I finally had the time to immerse myself in books again. It was an old acquaintance who suggested an online course in Cultural Studies. Initially it was daunting, but the syllabus was very accessible and the tutors incredibly supportive. This year I'm actually considering taking a degree course. There's no reason why not, despite my age.

2 Shortly after graduating, I started working for an IT start-up. The learning curve was massive, and everything seemed to be done at such a fast pace. We were developing algorithms that analysed the markets, and predicted emerging trends. You couldn't be risk averse … I found that it got very repetitive though, and I needed a bit more stimulation. So I attended pretty much every training course the company ran. Finance had always seemed like a foreign language, but within a few months I was pretty conversant with it. I suppose the key is decoding the jargon. Anyway, I looked at other avenues and there were a lot of lucrative contracts on the go. In terms of remuneration, it certainly outstrips IT work.

3 When I broached the subject of transferring here on a long-term basis, the college intimated that I'd need to improve my language proficiency – that was one condition that was necessary to meet for permanent residency to be granted. To help cut costs I stayed with a host family for a while. It was good to be in a supportive environment, and benefit from the opportunity to interact with native speakers daily. I got the grades I needed so was able to go ahead with the visa application. Since then I've had the confidence to take on a lot more challenges. They haven't all worked out, but you just have to take that in your stride and look on the bright side of things.

4 After several years of being together, we got to that point where we needed to know what was next: if it was going to be a lifelong thing, or would just peter out. We talked about getting married, but a wedding would've blown our meagre savings pretty quickly. When he mentioned family, I was taken aback. I thought about what would change if I became a mum. I'd lose that sense of camaraderie from work and there'd be fewer nights out with the girls. Despite my concerns, it's been so worthwhile. You get to know a whole new group of people, and there's a support network with new mums that is really life-affirming. I feel more grounded, like I belong here now.

5 I'd consider myself the kind of person who thrives on setting themselves targets, and I felt that the trip abroad would be a useful way of incorporating and developing some field research into what I've been doing. Given that the language barrier was a potential hazard, I enrolled on an intensive course and it turns out that I'm quite adept. I'd always favoured the scientific route, but evidently languages are my forte. Six months later on the Mandarin course and I'm going from strength to strength.

UNIT 8 Recording 2

A: Have you heard about these plans to stop prescribing antibiotics for common illnesses?

B: Yeah, there was something on the radio about it last week. Sounded quite interesting. The GP who was on said that limiting prescriptions could have a really positive effect on tackling drug-resistant superbugs.

A: Hmm. Well, I'm no expert but I think it's important that any risks are properly assessed before they make a big decision like that.

B: Really? What kind of risks could there possibly be? GPs aren't exactly renowned for doing anything that will endanger patients.

A: What about kids and elderly people though? They have a tough enough time as it is without succumbing to every bug that's doing the rounds.

B: Maybe it's just me, but it feels like dangers are always exaggerated. They're only talking about stopping dishing out pills for minor coughs and colds.

A: Well, I don't think people are ready for it yet. I'm guessing that a young parent with sick kids is going to feel very differently! What if they were denied treatment?

B: Listen, I don't really think it's an issue. We've got to move with the times. Think of the inordinate expense to the health services, and what'll happen when first-line antibiotics stop being effective.

A: Well, there are some things that I agree with, but I just think that this is probably a step too far.